Idiots, Hypocrites, Demagogues, and More Idiots

IDIOTS,
HYPOCRITES,
DEMAGOGUES,
AND
MORE IDIOTS

Not-So-Great Moments
in Modern American Politics

PAUL SLANSKY

BLOOMSBURY

NEW YORK · BERLIN · LONDON

Published by Bloomsbury USA, New York

All papers used by Bloomsbury USA are natural, recyclable products made from wood grown in well-managed forests. The manufacturing processes conform to the environmental regulations of the country of origin.

LIBRARY OF CONGRESS CATALOGING-IN-PUBLICATION DATA
HAS BEEN APPLIED FOR.

ISBN-10: 1-59691-375-4
ISBN-13: 978-1-59691-375-2

First U.S. Edition 2008

3   5   7   9   10   8   6   4

Typeset by Westchester Book Group
Printed in the United States of America by Quebecor World Fairfield

For Grace and her friends,
who'll have to clean up the mess
these people have made.

INTRODUCTION

"It's funny 'cause it's true."
—HOMER SIMPSON

Nowhere is the need to present a sanitized version of oneself greater than in politics. Ironically, the desperation that attaches to concealing one's flaws, prejudices, and honest opinions makes their eventual exposure inevitable. As Michael Kinsley wrote in the *New Republic* in 1984, "A 'gaffe' occurs not when a politician lies, but when he tells the truth."

This truth telling is always inadvertent, and just as invariably entertaining. The senator who was named the dumbest member of Congress moronically holds a press conference to say it's not true. The president who for years denied various accusations of marital infidelity has his DNA turn up on a White House intern's dress. The candidate who constantly referred to himself as "compassionate" can't keep a smile off his face whenever he hears the words "death penalty." Racism, sexism, religious prejudice, homophobia, xenophobia, sadism, criminality, alcoholism, incompetence, and, most relentlessly, stupidity are perpetually being revealed by people struggling to keep all of it hidden.

The rise of the political gaffe as a comedic art form can be attributed to two factors that arrived on the scene simultaneously: television and Richard M. Nixon. TV gave us a window into the personalities behind the people in power, and Nixon's was the weirdest personality ever seen. Wildly uncomfortable in his own skin, Nixon was the gaffe's pioneer, its first virtuoso, a man so aware—however subconsciously—that he deserved to be punished that he made self-destruction his life's work. This was apparent to anyone who watched his sweaty, stubbly visage during his first debate with John F. Kennedy in 1960, or witnessed the bleary-eyed bitterness on display two years later as he blamed reporters for his latest electoral defeat. One can only imagine children across America witnessing either event and shouting, "Mommy! Mommy! Bad man on TV!" Nixon's self-loathing was so boundless that he had to find the highest possible pinnacle—the presidency—to fling himself from. No less humiliation would do.

Watergate obliterated whatever remained of the notion that politicians were in any way better than us, and suddenly—with the concurrent emergence of gossip as a national industry—their foibles were fair game. A married congressman's drunken cavorting with a stripper, just the kind of thing that had formerly been hushed up, became a front-page story. A candidate's admission that he'd had lustful feelings he'd never acted upon led the evening news. When, in October of 1976, a cabinet official had to resign after telling a vulgar racist joke, the political gaffe established itself as a force to be reckoned with.

With the arrival of the twenty-four-hour cable news networks and all the C-SPANs, politicians were spending so much time in front of cameras and microphones that their opportunities to screw up increased exponentially. This up-close and ongoing scrutiny gave the stylish candidates an advantage over the merely substantive ones, thus empowering hordes of camera-friendly ignoramuses. The advent of political correctness raised the bar considerably as to what was deemed accept-able public discourse, yet hundreds, if not thousands, didn't get the memo. And now, the combination of cell-phone cameras and YouTube places every office holder and candidate at perpet-ual risk. For fans of political gaucherie, this is indeed the Golden Age.

The range of idiocy collected herein runs the gamut from the innocent tongue slip to the bigoted blurt, from denying having said something known to have been captured on tape to grinning broadly while being photographed for a mug shot, from inexcusably ignoring warnings of imminent disaster to terrorizing people into sacrificing their civil liberties and clos-ing their eyes to inhumanities conducted in their name. Some gaffes harm only the gaffer. Others hurt us all.

Two last things to remember: 1) There's nothing politi-cians hate more than ridicule; and 2) Everyone in this book has earned it.

Idiots, Hypocrites, Demagogues, and More Idiots

Vice presidential candidate **Dan Quayle** informed attendees at a 1988 campaign rally, "This election is about who's going to be the next president of the United States!"

———

Campaigning for the governorship of Illinois in 1982, **Adlai Stevenson III** declared, "I am not a wimp."

———

At a 1992 campaign stop, President **George Bush** told the crowd, "I don't want to run the risk of ruining what is a lovely recession." He meant to say "reception."

———

While taking part in a New Hampshire pancake-flipping contest during the 2000 primary campaign, **Gary Bauer** tossed one high in the air, caught it, and fell off the stage.

———

Campaigning in Iowa, President **Bill Clinton** told a 1996 college rally, "Since I was a little boy, I've heard about the Iowa caucuses," though the first one was held in 1972, when he was a toddler of twenty-five.

———

Speaking in 2000 at a New Hampshire school whose theme of the month was "Perseverance," candidate **George W. Bush** enthused, "This is preservation month. I appreciate preservation. It's what you do when you run for president. You've got to preserve."

━━

Roy Spence, media director for the 1984 Walter Mondale presidential campaign, praised his candidate because he "dares to be cautious."

━━

While briefly using the ruse of the 2000 presidential campaign to promote his latest self-congratulatory book, **Donald Trump** said, "I think the only difference between me and the other candidates is that I'm more honest and my women are more beautiful."

━━

Nebraska senator **Chuck Hagel**, the subject of much speculation regarding a possible campaign for the 2008 Republican presidential nomination, scheduled a much-anticipated "announcement on my political future." With reporters from all across the country gathered in Omaha and cable news networks broadcasting the March 2007 event live, Hagel declared, "I'm here today to announce that my family and I will make a decision on my political future later this year."

━━

A week after **Thomas Ravenel**, the South Carolina chairman of Rudy Giuliani's 2008 presidential campaign, was indicted on federal cocaine charges, the campaign released a list of state cochairs that included his father, **Arthur Ravenel**, who is best known for his 2000 reference to the NAACP as "the National Association of Retarded People," his subsequent apology to the retarded for equating them with the NAACP, and his 2006 complaint, after the incident had dogged him for six years, that "I made a rhetorical slip, and they want to lynch me for it."

A PASSIONATE ARGUMENT IN DEFENSE OF SOMETHING NO ONE OPPOSES

President **Gerald Ford**: "I say—and say it with emphasis and conviction—that homemaking is good for America. I say that homemaking is not out of date, and I reject strongly such accusations. Every American who chooses to be a homemaker can take pride in a fine, fine vocation. You should never be embarrassed to say anywhere on the face of this earth, 'I am an American homemaker, and I am proud of it.'"

16 THINGS PRESIDENT **RONALD REAGAN** DIDN'T KNOW

What His Only Black Cabinet Member Looked Like: When he saw Samuel Pierce, his secretary of housing and urban development, at a 1981 meeting of big-city mayors, he greeted him, "How are you, Mr. Mayor? I'm glad to meet you. How are things in your city?"

=

That There Were Still Segregated Schools in America: "I didn't know there were any," he said in 1982 about private schools that practiced discrimination. "Maybe I should have, but I didn't."

=

The Precise Identity of the Liberian Head of State: During a 1982 Rose Garden photo opportunity, he introduced Samuel K. Doe as "Chairman Moe."

=

That Jews Suffered More in Nazi Germany than Nazis Did: Defending his 1985 visit to the military cemetery at Bitburg, Germany, he said that Hitler's soldiers "were victims, just as surely as the victims in the concentration camps."

=

His Dog Millie's Name: During a 1981 vacation at his Santa Barbara ranch, reporters asked him what it was, and he replied, "Lassie."

=

That He Shouldn't Believe Everything He's Told: "I'm no linguist, but I have been told," he said in 1985, "that in the Russian language there isn't even a word for freedom." The word is "svoboda."

=

That He Made Training Films in Hollywood During World War II and Never Left the Country: He twice claimed to have been a photographer in an army unit filming the Nazi death camps, and had saved a copy of the film, and had shown it to a family member who asked if the conditions there had really been that bad.

=

Where He Was and Where He Was Going: At a 1982 dinner welcoming him to Brazil, he offered a toast to "the people of Bolivia." He then explained that Bolivia was the next stop on his trip, though he was actually going to Colombia and was not scheduled to visit Bolivia at all. On his return to the U.S., he told reporters, "Well, I learned a lot. You'd be surprised. They're all individual countries."

=

That the Guy He Was Campaigning for Wasn't a Bullet-Headed Insult Comic: At a 1986 Oklahoma rally for Sen. Don Nickles, he urged his audience to vote for "Don Rickles."

=

Some of the Fine Points of Jurisprudence in the United Kingdom: In 1982 he told a group of schoolchildren about a British law under which anyone carrying a gun while committing a crime was automatically tried for murder, whether or not the gun was used. When it was pointed out that no such law had ever been on the books in England, his spokesman Larry Speakes said, "Well, it's a good story, though." Four years later, in an interview with the *New York Times,* the president told the story again, and, of course, none of the three reporters present called him on it.

=

That the Three Republican Congressmen Visiting Him in 1983 Had Been Defeated Six Months Earlier: He asked them, "Don't you fellows have to vote?"

━━

A Key Fact About Submarine-Launched Nuclear Missiles: In 1982, he said they "can be recalled" if they are fired in error. They cannot.

━━

Which Props Go with Which Jewish Holidays: Addressing a group of religious broadcasters in 1985, he spoke of looking north from the White House in December and seeing "the huge menorah celebrating the Passover season in Lafayette Park."

━━

Every Little Detail of His Filmography: Right after his first inauguration, he stopped by the office of House Speaker Tip O'Neill, who showed him the desk that had been used by Grover Cleveland. The new president claimed to have portrayed him in a movie, forcing O'Neill to explain that he had actually played Grover Cleveland Alexander, the baseball player, and not Grover Cleveland, the president.

━━

How Totally Dependent on Its Mother a Three-Month-Old Fetus Is: He said in 1982 that fetuses born this young "have lived to, the record shows, to grow up and be normal human beings," though in fact the record shows that such fetuses are no more than 3½ inches long, and not one has ever survived.

—

The Answer to a Simple Question About Arms Control: During a 1984 stay at his Santa Barbara ranch, he stood speechless for several seconds, nodding and grunting and shrugging, until his wife, standing next to him, ducked her head and muttered, "Doing everything we can." Thus cued, the leader of the free world declared, "We're doing everything we can."

GEORGE W. BUSH KNOWS WHO HE IS

"I'm the decider, and I decide what is best." (2006)
"I'm the Commander Guy." (2007)

6 COMMENTS THAT WOMEN WEREN'T HAPPY TO HEAR

With President Ronald Reagan and Soviet leader Mikhail Gorbachev holding their first summit in Geneva in 1985, Chief of Staff **Donald Regan** explained why the activities of their wives would be of special interest to female newspaper readers: "They're not going to understand throw-weights, or what is happening in Afghanistan, or what is happening in human rights. Some women will, but most women . . . would rather read the human interest stuff."

—

On a 1992 broadcast of the *700 Club*, **Pat Robertson** told the gals in his audience, "I know this is painful for the ladies to hear, but if you get married, you have accepted the headship of a man, your husband. Christ is the head of the household and the husband is the head of the wife, and that's the way it is, period."

—

Defending herself in 1992 against suggestions of possible conflicts of interest from her husband's having done business with the law firm she worked for when he was governor of Arkansas, **Hillary Clinton** pouted, "I suppose I could have stayed home and baked cookies and had teas, but what I decided to do was to fulfill my profession which I entered before my husband was in public life."

—

In 2004, House Majority Leader **Tom DeLay** opined, "A woman can take care of the family. It takes a man to provide structure. To provide stability. Not that a woman can't provide stability, I'm not saying that. . . . It does take a father, though."

—

Dismissing the 1991 incident at the Tailhook Association convention, in which navy aviators groped and fondled female officers, as "much ado about nothing," Minnesota governor **Jesse Ventura** said in a 1999 *Playboy* interview, "These are people who live on the razor's edge and defy death and do things where people die. They're not going to consider grabbing a woman's breast or buttock a major situation."

—

Vice presidential candidate **Dan Quayle** told an eleven-year-old girl he'd want her to have the baby if she was raped by her father. "You're a very strong woman," he said. "Though this would be a traumatic experience that you would never forget, I think that you would be very successful in life."

3 LIGHTHEARTED COMMENTS ABOUT FORCED SEX

Comparing his having to suffer bad weather on his ranch to enduring rape, Texas gubernatorial candidate **Clayton Williams** said in 1990, "If it's inevitable, just relax and enjoy it."

—

During a 1980 debate on a bill banning sexual harassment in the workplace, Connecticut state senator **Steven Casey** said, "I wish *I* were sexually harassed."

—

Savannah, GA, mayor **John Rousakis** said in 1991 that a rape victim who couldn't identify her attacker nonetheless knew he was a Democrat because she "never had it so good."

2 THREATS TO AMERICAN YOUTH UNCOVERED BY THE CHRISTIAN RIGHT

The *National Liberty Journal*—Rev. **Jerry Falwell**'s monthly newspaper—published a 1999 "PARENTS ALERT" claiming that *Teletubbies*, a public television show aimed at toddlers less than three years old, was "damaging to the moral lives of our children" by "role modeling the gay life style" through its character Tinky Winky. "He is purple—the gay pride color," the article pointed out, "and his antenna is shaped like a triangle—the gay pride symbol." And, to Falwell, that magic bag he carried looked mighty like a purse. Despite all of this, PBS chose not to take the show off the air.

—

Two days before Halloween 1982, *700 Club* host **Pat Robertson** told viewers, "I think we ought to close Halloween down. Do you want your children to dress up as witches? The Druids used to dress up like this when they were doing human sacrifice. . . . [Your children] are acting out Satanic rituals and participating in it, and don't even realize it." Despite all of this, trick-or-treating has continued to take place annually.

LEAST CONVINCING ARGUMENT
FOR BEING A SLUMLORD

"If I didn't own them, somebody else would."
> Reagan aide **Lyn Nofziger** in 1981, justifying his ownership of three Baltimore tenements. As for his tenants' complaints, he pointed out, "You can't expect people paying $150-a-month rent to be living in upper income housing."

4 SEEMINGLY FORGOTTEN QUOTES BY
PRESIDENTIAL CANDIDATE **GEORGE W. BUSH**

Criticizing the Clinton administration's Somalia policy, he said, "I don't think our troops ought to be used for what's called nation-building."

———

Commenting on President Clinton's involvement in Kosovo, he said, "Victory means exit strategy, and it's important for the president to explain to us what the exit strategy is."

———

Explaining the rationale behind his campaign, he said, "I've got a reason for running. I talk about a larger goal, which is to call upon the best of America.... I'm running for a reason.... You cannot lead America to a positive tomorrow with revenge on one's mind. Revenge is so incredibly negative.... And I tease people by saying, 'A leader, you can't say, follow me, the world is going to be worse.'" (Two years later he justified his imminent invasion of Iraq by saying, "After all, this is the guy who tried to kill my dad.")

—

Asked how he'd conduct foreign policy, he said, "If we're an arrogant nation, they'll view us that way. But if we're a humble nation, they'll respect us as an honorable nation."

8 THINGS **DAN QUAYLE** DID DURING THE WEEKS AFTER HIS INAUSPICIOUS DEBUT AS GEORGE BUSH'S RUNNING MATE

Addressing the California delegation at the Republican convention, he told them, "The real question for 1988 is whether we're going to go forward to tomorrow or past to the—to the back!"

—

He campaigned in Ohio and warned that America is "naked, absolutely nude to attack" by the Soviets.

—

He pointed to his seat on the Senate Armed Services Committee as proof that he was qualified to be president. "I got through a number of things in the area of defense," he said, "like showing the importance of cruise missiles and getting them more accurate so that we can have precise precision."

—

He talked about the superiority of his ticket's position on child-care issues, telling a Massachusetts audience, "We understand the importance of having the bondage between the parent and the child."

===

He told an Oklahoma audience that the Holocaust was "an obscene period in our nation's history," then—lest anyone think he thought we were responsible for it—explained that he meant "in this century's history," adding cryptically, "We all lived in this century. I didn't live in this century."

===

He campaigned in Arizona and promised, "We're going to have the best-educated American people in the world."

===

He told a California crowd how thrilled he was to be on the ticket with "George the Bush."

===

He looked back on the campaign after it was over and said that it had taught him to talk less. "Verbosity," he explained, "leads to unclear, inarticulate things."

2 AVOIDABLE CONFLAGRATIONS

In 1980, the radical black back-to-nature cult MOVE established a commune in a working-class neighborhood in Philadelphia where, over the course of the next five years, their profane political diatribes and unhygienic ways became an increasing nuisance to their surrounding neighbors. In 1985, efforts to arrest four members of the group led to a gun battle with police, which led to the dropping of explosives on the cult's headquarters, which ignited an inferno that destroyed sixty-one homes and killed eleven people. In retrospect, Mayor **Wilson Goode** said the strategy was "perfect, except for the fire."

After the FBI ended its seven-week-long 1993 siege of the Branch Davidian cult's complex near Waco, TX, by tear-gassing the building and igniting a blaze that resulted in the deaths of some eighty people, a quarter of them children, Attorney General **Janet Reno** said of the decision to move in, "Based on what we know now, it was obviously wrong."

HOW WE GOT HERE

With George W. Bush slightly ahead in the latest vote tallies and the clock running out on the 2000 recount, Florida secretary of state (and cochairman of the state's Bush campaign) **Katherine Harris**, eager to shut things down before Al Gore might turn out to have won, said, "I do not believe the possibility of affecting the outcome of the election is enough to justify ignoring a statutory deadline."

MOST DELICIOUS UNREMARKED-UPON IRONY

In a *Los Angeles Times* special section recapping the five-week Florida recount, the sole advertiser was Banana Republic.

HOW WE GOT HERE AGAIN

In Alexandra Pelosi's HBO documentary *Diary of a Political Tourist*, New York representative **Peter King** was filmed at a 2003 White House barbecue boasting about the upcoming presidential election: "It's already over. The election's over. We won." Asked how he knew that Bush would win more than a year before the votes were cast, King said, "It's all over but the counting. And we'll take care of the counting."

15 COMMUNICATIONS INSPIRED BY
HURRICANE KATRINA

"I must say, this storm is much bigger than anyone expected."

FEMA Director **Michael Brown**, who'd spent much of his time in New Orleans as the hurricane hit e-mailing colleagues with messages like, "Can I quit now? Can I go home?" and complaining about the unfashionableness of his official FEMA storm attire.

—

"It looks like a lot of that place could be bulldozed."

House Speaker **Dennis Hastert**, arguing against spending money to rebuild New Orleans.

—

"It's totally wiped out. . . . It's devastating, it's got to be doubly devastating on the ground."

George W. Bush, looking out the window of *Air Force One* during his flyover of New Orleans.

—

"Considering the dire circumstances that we have in New Orleans, virtually a city that has been destroyed, things are going relatively well."

Michael Brown, at a point when tens of thousands who lacked food, water, and medication were packed into the inconceivably squalid convention center or clung to rooftops or huddled on bridges and overpasses as corpses floated in the stinking flood waters. Brown felt everything was copacetic because he'd "had no reports of unrest, if the connotation of the word 'unrest' means that people are beginning to riot, or, you know, they're banging on walls and screaming and hollering or burning tires or whatever. I've had no reports of that."

—

"We just learned of [the grim situation at] the convention center—'we' being the federal government—today."
Michael Brown to ABC's Ted Koppel, who asked incredulously, "Don't you guys watch television? Don't you guys listen to the radio? Our reporters have been reporting on it for more than just today."

—

"Brownie, you're doing a heck of a job."
George W. Bush, offering absurdly undeserved praise as he visited the devastated Gulf Coast area, where he tried to make America feel sorry for poor Mississippi senator **Trent Lott**, who "lost his entire house."

—

"Louisiana is a city that is largely under water."
Homeland Security head **Michael Chertoff**.

—

"Please roll up the sleeves of your shirt . . . all shirts. Even the President rolled his sleeves to just below the elbow. In this crises and on TV you just need to look more hard-working . . . ROLL UP THE SLEEVES!"
E-mail from **Sharon Worthy** to her boss, **Michael Brown**.

———

"I mean, you have people who don't heed those warnings and then put people at risk as a result of not heeding those warnings. There may be a need to look at tougher penalties on those who decide to ride it out and understand that there are consequences to not leaving."

Pennsylvania senator **Rick Santorum**, about whom Nebraska senator Bob Kerrey once said, "Santorum, that's Latin for 'asshole,'" apparently feeling that those whose utter poverty prevented them from any means of escape had not suffered enough.

———

"This wasn't about me going to my house. It was about me going to my district."

Louisiana representative **William Jefferson**, trying to justify using National Guard troops to retrieve his laptop and other belongings from his New Orleans home, thus making the troops unavailable for rescuing people clinging to rooftops or huddling in feces-strewn facilities. Two years later he was indicted on sixteen counts of various charges connected with taking as much as a million dollars worth of bribes.

———

"I really didn't hear that at all today. People came up to me all day long and said 'God bless your son,' people of different races, and it was very, very moving and touching, and they felt like when he flew over, that it made all the difference in their lives, so I just don't hear that."

Barbara Bush on *Larry King Live*, dismissing rapper Kanye

West's observation that "George Bush doesn't care about black people."

—

"Why would I do that?"

George W. Bush, dismissing California representative Nancy Pelosi's urging to fire Michael Brown. "I said, 'because of all that went wrong, of all that didn't go right last week,'" Pelosi said. "And he said, 'What didn't go right?'"

—

"I also want to encourage anybody who was affected by Hurricane Corina to make sure their children are in school."

Laura Bush, *getting the name of the hurricane wrong* while speaking to Mississippi parents.

—

"Now tell me the truth, boys. Is this kind of fun?"

Texas representative **Tom DeLay**, chatting with three young New Orleans evacuees having the time of their lives resting on cots in Houston's Reliant Park after having lost their homes.

—

"I'm going to go home and walk my dog and hug my wife, and maybe get a good Mexican meal and a stiff margarita and a full night's sleep."

Michael Brown, on his way back to Washington after being relieved of his Katrina-related duties.

LEAST ENTHUSIASTIC ENDORSEMENT SINCE DWIGHT EISENHOWER WAS ASKED WHAT MAJOR DECISIONS HIS VICE PRESIDENT, RICHARD NIXON, HAD BEEN INVOLVED IN AND ANSWERED, "IF YOU GIVE ME A WEEK, I MIGHT THINK OF ONE"

Asked whether he thought that vice presidential candidate Dan Quayle was qualified to be "a heartbeat away" from the presidency, Kansas senator **Bob Dole** answered, "Is he qualified compared to who? You can always find someone who's better in any business or profession."

3 DIGESTIVE MISHAPS

In 1981, New York City mayor **Ed Koch** was saved by the Heimlich maneuver in a Chinatown restaurant when he began choking after stuffing pork into his mouth while talking nonstop. Koch, fearful of offending Jewish voters with his nonkosher cuisine, lied and claimed it was sautéed watercress. Two years later, he ate and drank so much at an Italian restaurant that he passed out in the men's room.

While watching a 2002 NFL playoff game, **George W. Bush** fainted, toppled off a sofa, smacked his head on a coffee table, and bruised his cheek and lower lip after choking on a pretzel.

4 UNINTELLIGIBLE STATEMENTS

"Well, I think we need a foreign policy which is tied to our national security interests, which are tied to intelligent interests for the United States, that are tied to energy interests, which are tied to a sound economy here in the United States and an energy policy that is going to free us from heavy dependence to the Persian Gulf countries and to OPEC, which is strongly, which has the strength and the support of the American people, and which is predictable and certain, which has a down side to it in terms of disincentives to the Soviet Union for actions which are contrary to the, uh, to, uh, a standard of both international behavior and also has incentives to the Soviet Union, uh, to try to work in ways that can at least some, uh, create at least a world which is going to be freer from, uh, the nuclear nightmare which hangs over the world."

> Massachusetts senator **Ted Kennedy**, trying to wrest the 1980 Democratic presidential nomination away from Jimmy Carter.

—

"Having said that, I am, I thought, and maybe, again, I may be the only one with this dilemma, but I thought that originally the purpose of the agreement that is in dispute, whether the agreement is, as characterized by Senator Packwood's counsel, at some point, I guess, if this goes to court, he is going to contest the characterization of the agreement they made as unanimously characterized by the committee."

> Delaware senator **Joe Biden**, during a 1993 floor debate over subpoenaing Oregon senator Bob Packwood's diaries.

—

"Why wouldn't an enhanced deterrent, a more stable peace, a better prospect to denying the ones who enter conflict in the first place to have a reduction of offensive systems and an introduction to defensive capability. I believe that is the route this country will eventually go."

> Vice presidential candidate **Dan Quayle**, having set aside his prepared speech in favor of winging it, examining theories of nuclear deterrence in Chicago, where he also said, "[Indiana basketball coach] Bobby Knight told me this: 'There is nothing that a good defense cannot beat a better offense.' In other words a good offense wins."

—

"Well, it's an unimaginable honor to be the president during the Fourth of July of this country. It means what these words say, for starters. The great inalienable rights of our country. We're blessed with such values in America. And I—it's—I'm a proud man to be the nation based upon such wonderful values. . . . But the true greatness of America are the people."

> **George W. Bush** in 2001, explaining what Independence Day meant to him.

2 HORSEMEN OF THE APOCALYPSE

Testifying before the House Interior Committee in 1981 about the need to preserve natural resources for future generations, Ronald Reagan's antienvironmental Interior secretary **James Watt**—whose statement of purpose upon assuming his post was, "We will mine more, drill more, cut more timber"—observed, "I do not know how many future generations we can count on before the Lord returns."

———

In 1983, President **Ronald Reagan** observed that "[Not] until now has there ever been a time in which so many of the prophecies are coming together. There have been times in the past when people thought the end of the world was coming, and so forth, but never anything like this."

II MUCH-NEEDED CLARIFICATIONS

During Ronald Reagan's first year in the White House, California state senator and John Birch Society member **John G. Schmitz** warned that if Congress failed to enact the president's economic programs, the country would go so far down the tubes that "the best we could probably hope for is a military coup or something like that." "The best we could hope for is a military coup?" a stunned interviewer asked. "A good military coup," explained Schmitz. "Not a bad military coup, a *good* military coup."

———

As part of the FBI's 1979–80 Abscam sting, Florida representative **Richard Kelly** was caught on tape taking a $25,000 bribe from agents posing as Arab sheiks, stuffing it into his pockets, smoothing the bulges, and asking, "Does it show?" Kelly explained that he only took the money because he thought the undercover agents were "shady characters" and had decided to conduct his own investigation because "I wanted to know what these cats were up to." And why did he spend some of the cash, which he kept in his glove compartment? He wanted to make those cats think he was "on the hook." Kelly stuck to this story on the witness stand during his bribery trial, was rewarded with a guilty verdict, and ultimately spent thirteen months in prison.

———

Pennsylvania representative **Michael "Ozzie" Myers**, another Abscam stingee, was caught on tape telling undercover FBI agents, "Money talks and bullshit walks," while pocketing $50,000. At his trial, his lawyer, Plato Cacheris, explained that his client had merely been "play-acting," with a performance so convincing that it "would put Dustin Hoffman to shame." Though Myers—who once got into a fistfight with a waiter whom he felt to be insufficiently respectful to a member of Congress—made a post-conviction prediction that "the American people will never stand still for what the FBI did to me," the populace turned out to be utterly sanguine about it, and Myers—whose refusal to resign from Congress resulted in his being the first member since 1861 to be expelled—served twenty months in prison.

———

Accused in 1984 of having attacked Judaism as a "gutter religion," Black Muslim minister **Louis Farrakhan** said he had actually called it a "dirty religion."

———

Geraldine Ferraro, the 1984 Democratic vice presidential candidate, said that her husband John "did nothing wrong" by borrowing $100,000 from the account of an incapacitated woman whose estate he was managing because he "never knew it was improper."

—

Denying that the choice of U.S. treasurer Katherine Ortega to deliver the 1984 Republican convention's keynote speech was an effort to pander to women, an **unnamed party official** explained, "Ortega wasn't chosen because she's a woman. She was chosen because she's a Hispanic."

—

Feeling that the story about his disciplining himself as a child by eating rats—a story that was only out there because he'd put it in his 1980 autobiography—had grown out of proportion, Watergate burglar **G. Gordon Liddy** explained five years later that he "only ate the left hind quarter. Of one rat."

—

While answering phone calls from viewers on a 1978 Paris TV show, **Richard Nixon** told a caller who brought up Watergate, "I wasn't lying. I said things that later on seemed to be untrue."

—

Testifying before Congress at the 1987 Iran-contra hearings, Lt. Col. **Oliver North** explained, "I wasn't lying. I was presenting a different version from the facts."

—

Having switched from a pro-life to pro-choice position on abortion as he began his quixotic race for the 2004 Democratic presidential nomination, Ohio representative **Dennis Kucinich** explained, "The position I'm taking now is an expansion, it's not a reversal."

Explaining the difference between Americans and terrorists, **George W. Bush** said in 2003, "They hate things. We love things."

II MORE MUCH-NEEDED CLARIFICATIONS

Having been named New York City's first black deputy mayor in 1973, **David Dinkins** withdrew four weeks later when it became known that he hadn't filed income tax returns for the previous four years. "I haven't committed a crime," he explained. "What I did was fail to comply with the law."

Louisiana governor **Edwin Edwards** said of campaign contributions he accepted from large corporations in 1971, "Well, maybe it was illegal for them to give, but not for me to receive."

In a 2002 interview with the *Los Angeles Times*, Attorney General **John Ashcroft** explained, "Islam is a religion in which God requires you to send your son to die for Him. Christianity is a faith in which God sends His son to die for you."

In the wake of the riots outside the 1968 Democratic convention, Chicago mayor **Richard J. Daley** said, "Get the thing straight once and for all. The policeman isn't there to create disorder. The policeman is there to preserve disorder."

Though former House majority leader **Tom DeLay** admitted to having had numerous extramarital affairs in his 2007 book *No Retreat, No Surrender,* he attacked then–House Speaker Newt Gingrich for hypocritically carrying on an adulterous affair while leading the impeachment proceedings against Bill Clinton. And why wasn't the rabidly pro-impeachment DeLay equally hypocritical? "I was no longer committing adultery by that time," he explained. "There's a big difference."

President **John F. Kennedy**'s famous 1963 declaration of identification with Germans, "Ich bin ein Berliner," actually translated to "I am a jelly doughnut."

In a 1980 interview with Barbara Walters, ex-president **Richard Nixon** gave his assessment of his ex–vice president **Spiro Agnew**'s bribe-taking. "What was involved were the kickbacks while he was governor of Maryland," Nixon explained. "Some of the money was paid after he was in the White House, but the money was not for anything he had done as vice president."

A week later, Walters interviewed Agnew, who proceeded to corroborate the description of him by the court that disbarred him ("morally obtuse") by saying, "There's nothing wrong with [taking bribes] as long as you can't do anything for the guy." Asked if he would recommend politics as a career, he said no, because "the expectation of people from people in public office is just so high that no ordinary man can ever perform to suit them." (Translation: My God, they expect us not to take bribes!) And, asked if voters should be able to expect honesty from politicians, he answered, "Yes, but honesty is a different thing to different people."

Vice presidential candidate **Dan Quayle** explained that he was incapable during his debate with Lloyd Bentsen of telling the audience what he'd do if he suddenly became president because, "I had not had that question before."

Days later, he assured reporters, "Certainly I know what to do and when I am vice president—and I will be—there will be contingency plans under different situations. And I'll tell you what—I'm not going to go out and have a news conference about it, I'm going to put it in a safe and keep it there! Does that answer the question?"

Explaining in 1984 why he called himself a Texan even though he was born in Massachusetts, grew up in Connecticut, lived in Washington, and paid taxes in Maine, Vice President **George Bush** said, "I'm legally and every other way, emotionally, entitled to be what I want to be and that's what I want to be and that's what I am."

On his 2007 publicity tour for his book *At the Center of the Storm*, former CIA director **George Tenet** explained that though the popular belief is that he leapt about the Oval Office, exhorting that finding weapons of mass destruction in Iraq would be a "slam dunk," what he really said would be a "slam dunk" was making the gullible American populace *believe* there were weapons of mass destruction there.

———

Pennsylvania senator **Rick Santorum** explained in a 2003 interview, "I have no problem with homosexuality. I have a problem with homosexual acts." When asked if that meant that homosexuals shouldn't have sex, he brought up a Texas sodomy law case then pending before the Supreme Court and argued that the Constitution did not guarantee the right to privacy, and that if it did we could wind up in a world that condoned not only homosexuality but also polygamy, adultery, and "man on child, man on dog, or whatever the case may be." The reporter said, "I'm sorry, I didn't think I was going to talk about 'man on dog' with a United States senator, it's sort of freaking me out."

MAN ON DOG

"It has been said by some cynic, maybe it was a former president, 'If you want a friend in Washington, get a dog.' Well, we took them literally—that advice—as you know. But I didn't need that because I have Barbara Bush."
President **George Bush**, 1989.

8 INTERESTING THEORIES

In 1973, Richard Nixon's chief of staff **Alexander Haig** posited a "devil theory" that the mysterious $18\frac{1}{2}$ minutes of silence on a potentially incriminating Watergate-related tape recording was caused by "some sinister force."

—

In 1982, Pentagon official **Thomas K. Jones** offered a plan for surviving a nuclear attack: "Dig a hole, cover it with a couple of doors and then throw three feet of dirt on top. It's the dirt that does it. Everybody's going to make it if there are enough shovels to go around."

—

In 1982, antifeminist **Phyllis Schlafly** said, "Sex education is a principal cause of teenage pregnancy."

—

In a 2005 conversation with a caller on his *Morning in America* radio show, **William Bennett** posited, "[I]f you wanted to reduce crime . . . you could abort every black baby in this country, and your crime rate would go down." He described his speculation as a "thought experiment," complaining that he'd been "selectively quoted" in a way that "distorted my meaning," but his radio show was canceled within days.

—

"It causes a lot of people, including me, great distress to see judges use the authority that they have been given to make raw political or ideological decisions. . . . We have seen some recent episodes of courthouse violence in this country. . . . And I wonder whether there may be some connection between the perception in some quarters, on some occasions, where judges are making political decisions yet are unaccountable to the public, that it builds up and builds up and builds up to the point where some people engage in, engage in violence."

Texas senator **John Cornyn**, reacting to two 2005 incidents—one in which an accused rapist escaped from a deputy and shot four people to death, including the judge, and another in which the loser in a medical malpractice suit killed the husband and mother of the judge who ruled against him—by seeming to suggest that activist judges may just be asking for it with their incendiary rulings, though neither of the instances cited had anything to do with judicial overreaching, and even if they had, so what?

Speculating about just what the Watergate burglars had been looking for when they broke into the headquarters of the Democratic National Committee in 1972, Indiana representative **Earl Landgrebe** said, "Isn't it just possible that they were looking for a lead to who was financing those 100,000 peace demonstrators who finally forced, after Nixon was thrown out, the U.S. to surrender all of Southeast Asia to the Goddamn Communists who are over there slitting throats and tearing women apart!"

Secretary of State **Alexander Haig** suggested that four American nuns shot to death in El Salvador in 1981 might have been killed while trying to "run a roadblock."

Before the bodies of murdered civil rights workers Andrew Goodman, James Chaney, and Michael Schwerner were found in Neshoba County, Mississippi, in the summer of 1964, Sen. **James O. Eastland** called their disappearance "a publicity stunt" and opined that they were really in Cuba hanging out with Fidel Castro.

10 POLITICANS WHO EXPERIMENTED WITH MARIJUANA AND ONE WHO DIDN'T

New York mayor **Ed Koch** said he did it once "like everybody else, to see what it was like." He claimed not to have liked it.

—

Georgia representative **Newt Gingrich** said he smoked it once, but "it didn't have any effect on me."

—

Tennessee senator **Al Gore** said he smoked it "several times" in college and in Vietnam but "it did not become a significant part of my life." (Asked, on a 2000 MTV special about the college years of the candidates, whether he "chose to" smoke pot as a youth, he answered, "Well, I don't think anyone *made* you smoke.")

—

Rhode Island senator **Claiborne Pell** said he smoked it "many years ago" but "didn't like it and never tried it again."

—

Former Arizona governor **Bruce Babbitt** said he smoked it "back in the sixties, in a culture of widespread use."

—

Florida senator **Lawton Chiles** smoked it "once in private over seventeen years ago, and I never tried it again."

—

Florida representative **Connie Mack**, after having denied it for years, said he smoked it "more than once, but not often."

—

Presidential candidate **Bill Clinton** said, "When I was [at school] in England, I experimented with marijuana a time or two, and I didn't like it, and I didn't inhale, and I didn't try it again."

—

New Jersey governor **Christine Todd Whitman** said, "Unlike the president, I inhaled. And then I threw up."

—

New York mayoral candidate **Mike Bloomberg** said, "You bet I did, and I enjoyed it."

—

Resigned president **Richard Nixon**'s spokesman, John Taylor, said his boss "has never smoked pot." Asked how he knew, Taylor said, "I just feel absolutely certain about it. Don't you?"

LEAST GARRULOUS JUSTICE IN THE HISTORY OF THE SUPREME COURT

After speaking a mere 281 words over the course of the two preceding terms, **Clarence Thomas** sat through the entire 2006–2007 term without uttering a syllable.

BEST EXAMPLE OF PROTESTING TOO MUCH

Texas representative **Dick Armey** claimed that his 1995 reference to Barney Frank (his gay House colleague from Massachusetts) as "Barney Fag" was a mere slip of the tongue, "nothing more than the unintentional mispronunciation of another person's name that sounded like it was something that it was not." Not content to offer this absurd excuse for his offense, he went on to paint himself as the victim, attacking the media for even reporting the story. "To have my five children or anybody else's five children turn on their TV today and see a transcript of a mispronunciation on the air as if I had no sense of decency, cordiality, or even good manners is unacceptable and is an act in itself that is indecent." Five years later, when the homosexual-obsessed congressman said, "I'm Dick Armey. And if there is a dick army, Barney Frank would want to join up," he at least had the decency not to claim misquotation.

14 HOMOPHOBES HATING

California representative **Randy "Duke" Cunningham** said in 1998 that the rectal exam that checks for prostate cancer was "just not natural, unless maybe you're Barney Frank."

In 1989, California representative **William Dannemeyer**—apparently convinced that the only reason the entire heterosexual community doesn't share his obsessive revulsion toward homosexuality is because they're unaware of the graphic details—inserted an entry entitled "What Homosexuals Do," into the *Congressional Record*. This was the first time that descriptions of rimming, golden showers, and fisting—and a list of the kinds of things that get inserted into rectums—appeared there. (The following year, he addressed the House on the subject of sodomy laws, referring at one point to "a case with the ironic name of Hardwick.")

Dannemeyer's lunacy extended beyond his fanatical homophobia after he left office in 1992. Two years later, he futilely demanded that Congress look into the "frightening" number of people—twenty-four, he claimed—with a connection to Bill Clinton who died "under other than natural circumstances." And in 2006, he read a book by a member of the Scott Peterson defense team and became convinced that "a grave injustice has been done." According to Dannemeyer, Laci Peterson was killed not by her psychopathic husband, but rather by "a satanic cult operating in this state."

Reverend **Jerry Falwell** preached, "AIDS is not just God's punishment for homosexuals. It is God's punishment for the society that tolerates homosexuals." On another occasion he called homosexuals "brute beasts . . . part of a vile and satanic system [that] will be utterly annihilated, and there will be a celebration in heaven."

—

Presidential hopeful **Gary Bauer** called a 1999 Vermont Supreme Court decision recognizing homosexual couples "worse than terrorism."

—

Fearful that a 1977 Miami law prohibiting discrimination against gays would allow homosexuals to "recruit our children" into their sordid lifestyle, singer and Florida orange juice spokesperson **Anita Bryant** led the "Save Our Children" campaign that managed to get the law repealed. "If gays are granted rights," Bryant warned, "next we'll have to give rights to prostitutes and to people who sleep with St. Bernards and to nail biters."

—

In 1995, Montana state senator **Al Bishop** described gay sex as "even worse than" rape.

—

In 1992, **Pat Robertson** told his *700 Club* audience, "It's one thing to say, 'We have rights to jobs . . . we have rights to be left alone in our little corner of the world to do our thing.' It's an entirely different thing to say, 'Well, we're . . . going to go into the schools and we're going to take your children and your grandchildren and turn them into homosexuals.' Now that's wrong."

⸺

Following a 1992 sermon in which Georgia reverend **Len B. Tucker** condemned homosexuality as "satanic," Vice President **Dan Quayle** praised the minister's "very positive message."

⸺

In 1985, Houston mayoral candidate **Louie Welch** was caught on an unexpectedly open microphone suggesting that one way to halt the spread of AIDS "is to shoot the queers."

⸺

North Carolina senator **Jesse Helms** announced that he would try to block the 1993 nomination of openly gay Roberta Achtenberg to be an assistant secretary at the Department of Housing and Urban Development "because she's a damn lesbian. I'm not going to put a lesbian in a position like that. If you want to call me a bigot, fine."

⸺

During a 2006 Senate debate about an amendment to ban gay marriage, Oklahoma senator **James Inhofe** held up a photo of his family and said, "My wife and I have been married forty-seven years. We have twenty kids and grandkids. I'm really proud to say that in the recorded history of our family, we've never had a divorce or any kind of homosexual relationship."

⸺

Oklahoma representative **Tom Coburn**, who had previously distinguished himself by attacking NBC for broadcasting *Schindler's List* ("with full-frontal nudity, violence, and profanity"), warned in 2004 that "Lesbianism is so rampant in some of the schools in southeast Oklahoma that they'll only let one girl go to the bathroom. Now think about it. Think about that issue. How is it that that's happened to us?"

During his 2004 campaign for the Illinois Senate seat won by Barack Obama, **Alan Keyes** told an interviewer that homosexuality was based on "selfish hedonism." Asked if that meant Dick Cheney's gay daughter Mary was a selfish hedonist, Keyes said, "Of course she is. That goes by definition. Of course she is." He went on to explain why gay sex wasn't really sex: "It is the mutual pursuit of pleasure through the stimulation of the organs intended for procreation, but it has nothing to do with sexuality because they are of the same sex. . . . The sexual difference does not exist. They are therefore not having sexual relations." Amusingly, Keyes's own daughter, Maya, came out publicly a few months later.

In 1971, President **Richard Nixon** was telling his aides **H. R. Haldeman** and **John Ehrlichman** about an episode of a TV show he'd seen that he thought was called "Archie's Guys." (It was actually *All in the Family.*)

As he described it, "Archie is sitting here with his hippie son-in-law, married to the screwball daughter. The son-in-law apparently goes both ways. This guy [comes in]. He's obviously queer, wears an ascot, but not offensively so. Very clever. Uses nice language. Shows pictures of his parents. . . .

"I don't mind the homosexuality," the president assured his aides, lest they think he was some kind of bigot. "I understand it. The point that I make is that, goddamn it, I do not think that you glorify on public television homosexuality. You don't glorify it, John, any more than you glorify, uh, whores. . . . I don't want to see this country go that way. You know what happened to the Greeks! Homosexuality destroyed them. Sure, Aristotle was a homo, we all know that, so was Socrates. . . . Do you know what happened to the Romans? The last six Roman emperors were fags. . . . The Catholic Church went to hell, three or four centuries ago. It was homosexual, and it had to be cleaned out. That's what's happened to Britain, it happened earlier to France. . . .

"Look at this country. You think the Russians allow dope? Homosexuality, dope, immorality are the enemies of strong societies. That's why the communists and left-wingers are clinging to one another. They're trying to destroy us." He brought up northern California and said, "You know what's happened."

"San Francisco has just gone clear over," Ehrlichman said.

"But it's not just the ratty part of town," said Nixon. "The upper class in San Francisco is that way. The Bohemian Grove [an elite, secret gathering north of the city], which I attend from time to time. It is the most faggy goddamned thing you could ever imagine, with that San Francisco crowd. I can't shake hands with anybody from San Francisco."

2 CONGRESSMEN WHO FAILED TO LEARN WHAT WOULD SEEM TO HAVE BEEN FAIRLY OBVIOUS LESSONS

In 1998, five days after Michael Kennedy was killed by skiing into a tree, California representative **Sonny Bono** was killed by . . . skiing into a tree.

━━

South Dakota representative **Bill Janklow**, who had received a dozen speeding tickets and had been involved in eight accidents, ran a stop sign at 70-plus miles per hour one night in 2003 and killed a motorcyclist.

4 EXAMPLES OF HOW SOMETIMES IT SEEMS LIKE TIME IS PASSING MORE THAN A HALF MILLION TIMES FASTER THAN IT ACTUALLY IS

On the occasion of her twenty-ninth wedding anniversary in 1981, First Lady **Nancy Reagan** noted, "It seems like twenty-nine minutes." A year later, she observed of her thirtieth anniversary, "It feels like thirty minutes." Two years later, she offered, "I cannot believe it's been thirty-two years. It seems like thirty-two minutes." And four years after that, "It seems like thirty-six minutes."

2 EXPLANATIONS FOR 9/11

"What we saw on Tuesday, as terrible as it is, could be minuscule if . . . God continues to lift the curtain and allow the enemies of America to give us probably what we deserve. . . . The ACLU's got to take a lot of blame for this . . . throwing God out of the public square, out of the schools. The abortionists have got to bear some burden for [9/11] because God will not be mocked. And when we destroy forty million little innocent babies, we make God mad. I really believe that the pagans and the abortionists and the feminists and the gays and the lesbians who are actively trying to make that an alternative lifestyle, the ACLU, People for the American Way—all of them who have tried to secularize America—I point the finger in their face and say, 'You helped this happen.' "

> Rev. **Jerry Falwell** to **Pat Robertson**, who said, "Well, I totally concur."

"We have a court that has essentially stuck its finger in God's eye and said we're going to legislate you out of the schools. We're going to take your commandments from off the courthouse steps in various states. We're not going to let little children read the commandments of God. We're not going to let the Bible be read, no prayer in our schools. We have insulted God at the highest levels of our government. And then we say, 'Why does this happen?' Well, why it's happening is that God Almighty is lifting his protection from us."

> **Pat Robertson.**

DON'T SAY WE WEREN'T WARNED

Troubled by the decision of Orlando, Florida, officials to display rainbow flags during Disney World's 1998 "Gay Days" event, **Pat Robertson** warned, "I don't think I'd be waving those flags in God's face if I were you. . . . [A] condition like this will bring about the destruction of your nation. It'll bring about terrorist bombs, it'll bring earthquakes, tornadoes, and possibly a meteor."

11 WHITE GUYS TALKING ABOUT BLACKS

In a 1971 conversation with aide John Ehrlichman taped in the Oval Office, President **Richard Nixon** said, "I have the greatest affection for them, but I know they're not going to make it for five hundred years. They aren't. . . . The Mexicans are a different cup of tea. They have a heritage. At the present time, they steal, they're dishonest. [But] they do have some concept of family life, they don't live like a bunch of dogs, which the Negroes do live like."

———

Campaigning for the mayoralty of Los Angeles in 1981, **Sam Yorty** complained, "The black people are really racist. They vote for black people because they are black."

———

On his return from a 1983 trip to Africa, **Charles Z. Wick**, director of the U.S. Information Agency, observed, "Some of them have marvelous minds, those black people over there."

Reagan appointee **Thomas Ellis**, who belonged to an all-white country club, spent time in—and had extensive holdings in—South Africa, and who directed a group that funded research into the genetic inferiority of blacks, nonetheless said, "I do not believe in my heart that I'm a racist."

Houston city councilman **Jim Westmoreland** suggested in 1989 that an alternative way to name an airport in honor of the late black representative Mickey Leland was to call it "Nigger International."

Speaking about the Black Panthers in 1971, Philadelphia mayor **Frank Rizzo** said, "They should be strung up. I mean, within the law."

During a 1995 interview on *Larry King Live*, North Carolina senator **Jesse Helms** got a call from a man who thanked him for "everything you've done to help keep down the niggers." Helms replied, "Well, thank you, I think."

Georgia governor **Lester Maddox**, famous for helping to make ax handles a symbol of segregation, declared, "That's part of American greatness, is discrimination. Yes, sir. Inequality, I think, breeds freedom and gives a man opportunity."

During a 1988 TV interview, House Minority Leader **Bob Michel** lamented the passing of minstrel shows from the national scene. "We used to have minstrel shows when I was in grade school, you know," he said. "Of course, today you can't do that, everybody blackfaced up." Still, it was obvious that he really, really missed them. "I used to love to imitate, for example, Kingfish and uh, Amos 'n' Andy," he said, proceeding to do just that. "We never thought of it in disparaging terms. It was just a part of life. And it was fun." Another problem, he added, was the way political correctness forced lyric changes in "Ol' Man River" and other songs of its ilk. "Now the original, you know, 'niggers,' it's offensive, so we don't use it," he said, complaining, "Now, some people just say 'some folks' [work on the river]. Well, gosh, 'some folks'? The point was, it was blacks were slaves and that was the, you know, that's the way it was. I don't see anything disparaging in that."

In October 1994, Montana senator **Conrad Burns**—who years earlier had stunned a group of civil rights lobbyists by inviting them to a charitable function he referred to as a "slave auction"—was asked by a constituent, "Conrad, how can you live back there [in Washington, D.C.] with all those niggers?" Burns just chuckled and replied, "It's a hell of a challenge."

Burns continued to plunge his feet into his mouth over the years, referring to Arabs as "ragheads," telling a woman afraid of losing her job that if she did, she could stay home and take care of her kids, and responding to a simple "How ya doing today, Senator?" with the unexpected rejoinder, "I'm ready to go get knee-walking drunk."

Interpreting this last faux pas, his spokesman explained,

"He basically said, 'I'm tired,' but he said it in a funny way. That is who he is." And who he was the morning after the 2006 election was a defeated senator.

———

Reminiscing about the good old days in 1998, a year before Gov. George W. Bush appointed him chairman of a Texas law enforcement commission, Marshall, Texas, police chief **Charles W. Williams** recalled, "Back then we had Nigger Charlie and Nigger Sam, Nigger Joe. And we regarded those people with all the respect in the world. That was their name. They didn't mind. It wasn't any big deal then." (Williams was also known to have used the terms "porch monkey" and "black bastard," but argued, "You just have to show me where it's a racial slur.")

2 THINGS THAT ARE JUST FANTASTIC, EXCEPT, OF COURSE, FOR THE PARTS THAT AREN'T SO FANTASTIC

In 2001, Secretary of the Treasury **Paul O'Neill** pointed out, "If you set aside Three Mile Island and Chernobyl, the safety record of nuclear power is really very good."

———

In 1989, Washington, D.C., mayor **Marion Barry** boasted, "Outside of the killings, we have one of the lowest crime rates in the country."

12 THINGS VICE PRESIDENT **DAN QUAYLE** DID DURING HIS FIRST YEAR IN OFFICE

He gloated that members of Bush's team who treated him with contempt during the campaign now had to deal with him. "I'm the vice president," he said. "They know it, and they know that I know it."

———

He visited a Chicago school and exhorted students, "We will move forward, we will move upward, and, yes, we will move onward."

———

He told a reporter for *U.S. News & World Report*, "Every once in a while, you let a word or phrase out and you want to catch it and bring it back. You can't do that. It's gone, gone forever."

———

He addressed the United Negro College Fund and misquoted its slogan—"A mind is a terrible thing to waste"—as "What a waste it is to lose one's mind or not to have a mind is being very wasteful. How true that is."

———

He was asked what the Bush administration stood for and replied, "This administration stands for the future. It also stands for what's good about this country."

———

He declared, "I believe we are on an irreversible trend toward more freedom and democracy—but that could change."

═══

He addressed the twentieth-anniversary celebration of the moon landing and said, "Welcome to President Bush, Mrs. Bush, and my fellow astronauts," though of course he was never an astronaut.

═══

He explained that he was in favor of sending humans to Mars because "Mars is essentially in the same orbit [as Earth]. Mars is somewhat the same distance from the sun, which is very important. We have seen pictures where there are canals, we believe, and water. If there is water, that means there is oxygen. If oxygen, that means we can breathe." (In fact, Mars, which is fifty million miles further from the sun than Earth, has no canals, water, or oxygen.)

═══

He told ABC's Sam Donaldson, "I stand by all the misstatements that I've made."

═══

He inspected earthquake-ravaged San Francisco, calling it a "heart-rendering sight" and adding, "The loss of life will be irreplaceable."

═══

He told CNN's Larry King, "One word sums up probably the responsibility of any vice president, and that one word is 'to be prepared.'"

For Christmas, he gave President George Bush a toilet paper holder that played "Hail to the Chief" when the paper was unrolled.

MOST ILL-ADVISEDLY BRAZEN FINGER WAG

At a 1998 White House event a week after the intern scandal broke, President **Bill Clinton** wagged his finger at the TV cameras and boldly declared, "I want to say one thing to the American people. I want you to listen to me. I'm going to say this again: I did not have sexual relations with that woman—Miss Lewinsky."

13 THINGS FORMER PONTIAC SALESMAN **EVAN MECHAM** DID AFTER BEING ELECTED GOVERNOR OF ARIZONA IN 1986 (AND BEFORE BEING INDICTED, IMPEACHED, AND REMOVED FROM OFFICE IN 1987)

He canceled the state's observance of Martin Luther King, Jr.'s birthday because "King doesn't deserve a holiday," telling a local black leader, "You folks don't need another holiday. What you folks need are jobs."

He demanded a list of all homosexuals in the state government.

=

He spoke at a John Birch Society convention.

=

He nominated a twice court-martialed man to investigate government corruption.

=

He referred to black children as "pickaninnies."

=

He told an audience in a synagogue that America is "a great Christian nation."

=

He reported that when he told Japanese golfers how many courses Arizona had, "suddenly they got round eyes."

=

He blamed working women for high divorce rates.

=

He hired an education adviser who said that if parents told their kids the world was flat, "the teacher doesn't have the right to try to prove otherwise."

=

He explained that the black people in his employ were there "because they are the best people who applied for the cotton-picking job."

—

When a reporter asked him for the "true version" of a controversial incident, he fumed, "Don't ever ask me for a true statement again!"

—

He came to believe he was being eavesdropped on by laser beams. "Whenever I'm in my house or my office, I always have a radio on," he said. "It keeps the lasers out."

—

He said, "I'm not sure but what maybe we have become a bit too much a democracy."

3 ALL-TOO-EASILY DISPROVED DENIALS

In 1982, Vice President **George Bush** denied that he'd ever used the phrase "voodoo economics" to describe Ronald Reagan's economic policies. NBC newsman Ken Bode promptly broadcast the two-year-old videotape.

—

In 2005, televangelist **Pat Robertson** denied that he'd called for the assassination of Venezuelan president Hugo Chavez, claiming that he'd been "misinterpreted by the AP, but that happens all the time." As this denial was issued, footage circulated on the Internet of him saying "You know, I don't know about this doctrine of assassination, but if he thinks we're trying to assassinate him, I think that we really ought to go ahead and do it. It's a whole lot cheaper than starting a war. . . . We have the ability to take him out, and I think the time has come that we exercise that ability."

——

In 1988, Utah senator **Orrin Hatch** denied calling the Democrats "the party of homosexuals." A radio station found the statement on tape.

2 CONSIDERED ASSESSMENTS

"I really think he's a Renaissance kind of guy, and I've known him for twenty years, and I've never been on a topic where he doesn't know something about it."

Cheney aide **Mary Matalin** on **George W. Bush**.

——

"This is one of the most intellectually gifted presidents we've had."

White House Senior Advisor **Karl Rove** on **George W. Bush**.

THE INTELLECTUALLY GIFTED
GEORGE W. BUSH

"When I was coming up, it was a dangerous world and you knew exactly who the 'they' were. It was us versus them, and it was clear who 'them' was. Today, we're not so sure who the 'they' are, but we know they're there." (2000)

—

"The California crunch really is the result of not enough power-generating plants and then not enough power to power the power of generating plants." (2001)

—

"And so, in my State of the—my State of the Union—or state—my speech to the nation, whatever you want to call it, speech to the nation—I asked Americans to give four thousand years—four thousand hours over the next—the rest of your life—of service to America. That's what I asked—four thousand hours." (2002)

—

"There's an old saying in Tennessee—I know it's in Texas, probably in Tennessee—that says 'Fool me once, shame on . . . shame on you. Fool me . . . you can't get fooled again.'" (2002)

—

"The war on terror involves Saddam Hussein, because of the nature of Saddam Hussein, the history of Saddam Hussein, and his willingness to terrorize himself." (2003)

LOWEST POLL RATING

In a 2005 Zogby poll, Ohio governor **Bob Taft**—having pleaded no contest to four misdemeanors having to do with undisclosed gifts—scored an approval rating of 6.5 percent.

6 WHO RESIGNED IN DISGRACE

On the day that Bill Clinton delivered his acceptance speech at the 1996 Democratic convention, his adviser **Dick Morris** resigned after the news broke that not only had he been seeing a prostitute and sucking her toes, but he'd been impressing her—*impressing a prostitute!*—by letting her listen in on his phone calls with the president.

National Security Advisor **Richard Allen** resigned in 1982 after taking $1,000 and two Seiko watches from Japanese journalists—on his first day on the job—for arranging an interview with First Lady Nancy Reagan. Drawing a line so fine that it couldn't be seen, Allen explained, "I didn't accept it. I received it."

Declaring, "My truth is that I am a gay American," New Jersey governor **James McGreevey** resigned in 2004 after admitting to having had an extramarital affair with Golan Cipel, whom he had appointed as his counterterrorism adviser despite the man's utter lack of credentials for such a crucial position.

═══

Speaker of the House **Jim Wright** resigned in 1989 after being accused of exceeding the allowable maximum in extra-congressional speaking fees and giving his wife a job that let them get around the allowable maximum in gifts.

═══

Interior Secretary **James Watt** resigned in 1983 after having boasted, of the diversity of his coal-leasing commission, "We have every kind of mixture you can have. I have a black, I have a woman, two Jews, and a cripple." Then, having resigned, he struck a crucifixion pose.

═══

Claude Allen, a George W. Bush aide who was earning $161,000 a year, resigned in 2006 after being arrested for refund theft, a scam in which items are fraudulently returned to stores.

7 STATEMENTS BY SECRETARY OF STATE **ALEXANDER HAIG** THAT, WHILE NOT AS MEMORABLE AS HIS SWEATY, WILD-EYED DECLARATION OF BEING "IN CONTROL" AT THE WHITE HOUSE AFTER REAGAN WAS SHOT, ARE NONETHELESS WORTH NOTING

"It is my view that the most careful caution should be applied."

═══

"I'll have to caveat my response, Senator."

———

"Not in the way you contexted it, Senator."

———

"I don't want to saddle myself with a statistical fence."

———

"The very act of definitizing an answer to this question undercuts the fundamental deterrent on which our peace and security rests."

———

"This is not an experience I haven't been through before."

———

"That's not a lie. It's a terminological inexactitude."

HOW TO MAKE OFF-SHORE DRILLING VISUALLY PALATABLE

Defending off-shore drilling in 1985, President **Ronald Reagan** offered a suggestion to pacify those who object to the sight of oil rigs off their beaches. "You've got that whole expanse of ocean. It isn't as if you were looking at the ocean through a little frame, and now somebody put something in the way," he said. "We've got a lot of freighters . . . up in mothball. Why don't we bring down some and anchor them between the shore and the oil derrick? And then the people would see a ship, and they wouldn't find anything wrong with that at all."

7 OBSERVATIONS ABOUT THE FAMILY

"Fathers have a unique and irreplaceable role in the lives of children."
   George W. Bush, 2001.

━━

"Don't forget about the importance of the family. It begins with the family. We're not going to redefine the family. Everybody knows the definition of the family. [meaningful pause] A child. [meaningful pause] A mother. [meaningful pause] A father. There are other arrangements of the family, but that is a family and family values."
   Vice presidential candidate **Dan Quayle**, 1988.

━━

"I mean a child that doesn't have a parent to read to that child or that doesn't see that when the child is hurting to have a parent and help out or neither parent there enough to pick the kid up and dust him off and send him back into the game at school or whatever, that kid has a disadvantage."
   President **George Bush**, 1992.

━━

"One third of the children today are born into homes without families."

Soon-to-be (and then soon-*not*-to-be) presidential candidate **Dan Quayle**, 1999.

———

"I know how hard it is for you to put food on your family."

Presidential candidate **George W. Bush**, 2000.

———

"I suppose three important things certainly come to my mind that we want to say thank you. The first would be our family. Your family, my family—which is composed of an immediate family of a wife and three children, a larger family with grandparents and aunts and uncles. We all have our family, whichever that may be. . . . The very beginnings of civilization, the very beginnings of this country, goes back to the family. And time and time again, I'm often reminded, especially in this presidential campaign, of the importance of a family, and what a family means to this country. And so when you pay thanks, I suppose the first thing that would come to mind would be to thank the Lord for the family."

Vice presidential candidate **Dan Quayle**, 1988.

———

"Families is where our nation finds hope, where wings take dream."

George W. Bush, 2000.

5 THINGS PEOPLE SAID THEY WEREN'T

Refusing to speculate about the possible recurrence of cancer on his nose, President **Ronald Reagan** explained in 1985, "I'm not medical."

⸺

Pleading "not guilty" to charges of illegal lobbying, longtime Reagan adviser **Lyn Nofziger** declared in 1987, "I am not a felon."

⸺

Promising that he would stick to a healthful diet after suffering a minor stroke in 1987, New York mayor **Ed Koch** declared, "I am not a wild man nor a schmuck."

⸺

In 1985, President **Ronald Reagan** revealed, "I'm not an intellectual."

10 STATEMENTS BY GEORGE W. BUSH'S SECRETARY OF DEFENSE **DONALD RUMSFELD**

"What we are doing is that which is doable in the way we're currently doing it." (2001)

⸺

"In Afghanistan, people who are friendly [to the United States] and unfriendly are constantly meeting together. Indeed, sometimes the same people can be friendly and later unfriendly within a relatively short period of time. There are also people who can pretend they're friendly and who, in fact, are not very friendly." (2002)

=

"There are known knowns. These are things we know that we know. There are known unknowns. That is to say, there are things that we know we don't know. But there are also unknown unknowns. There are things we don't know we don't know." (2002)

=

"I believe what I said yesterday. I don't know what I said, but I know what I think, and I assume it's what I said." (2002)

=

"If something is going to happen, there has to be something for it to happen with that's interested in having it happen." (2002)

=

"The plan [in Iraq] is to prevent a civil war, and, to the extent one were to occur, to have the, from a security standpoint, have the Iraqi security forces deal with it to the extent they're able to." (2006)

=

"The United States isn't going to do anything that it's not capable of doing. And if we do something, we'll be capable of doing it." (2002)

=

"I'm not into this detail stuff. I'm more concept-y." (2002)

—

"Death has a tendency to encourage a depressing view of war." (2004)

—

"Stuff happens!" (2003)

5 CONGRESSIONAL ALTERCATIONS

When New York representative **Thomas Downey** confronted California representative **Robert Dornan** in 1985 about Dornan's having called him "a draft-dodging wimp," Dornan grabbed him by the collar and tie and said, "It's good you're being protected by the sergeant at arms. If I saw you outside, it would be a different story." He later acknowledged having held on to Downey's tie, but only because "it was crooked and it needed to be straightened."

—

When Texas senator **John Cornyn** sniped at fellow senator (and presidential hopeful) **John McCain** for missing all but the last day of the 2007 debate on immigration reform, McCain shouted, "Fuck you! I know more about this than anyone else in the room."

—

Upon being told to "shut up" by Colorado representative **Scott McInnis** during a 2003 House debate on a pension bill, California representative **Pete Stark** shot back, "Oh, you think you are big enough to make me, you little wimp? Come on. Come over here and make me. I dare you. You little fruitcake. You little fruitcake. I said, you are a fruitcake."

⸺

A 2004 argument between Vermont senator **Patrick Leahy** and **Dick Cheney** about the latter's connections to the multinational corporation Halliburton ended with Cheney telling Leahy, "Go fuck yourself."

⸺

Furious at a U.S. Capitol police officer whose 2006 failure to recognize her she instantly attributed not to the fact that she wasn't wearing her identifying lapel pin but, rather, to racism, Georgia representative **Cynthia McKinney** punched him in the chest.

2 SHOCKED—SHOCKED!—LEGISLATORS

Admitting that he belonged to a private spa that was shut down as a house of prostitution, Iowa senator **Roger Jepsen** explained in 1984 that he thought it was a health club, he only went once, and anyway it all happened before his "commitment to Christ."

⸺

After getting caught in 1984 receiving a blow job in his car from a prostitute, California representative **Ken Calvert** explained that he didn't know she was a whore.

WORST RESPONSE TO A QUESTION
THAT THE DULLEST SIMPLETON SHOULD
HAVE BEEN EXPECTING

With the announcement of his challenge to President Jimmy Carter imminent, Massachusetts senator **Edward Kennedy** granted a 1979 interview to CBS's Roger Mudd in which Kennedy managed to prove himself incapable of answering the most easily prepared-for question imaginable. "Why do you want to be president?" Mudd predictably asked.

"Well," Kennedy said, "I'm—were I to—to make the—the announcement and—to run, the reasons that I would run is because I have a great belief in this country, that it is—has more natural resources than any nation in the world, has the greatest educated population in the world, the greatest capacity for innovation in the world, and the greatest political system in the world. And yet I see at the current time that most of the industrial nations of the world are exceeding us in terms of productivity, are doing better than us meeting the problems of inflation, that they're dealing with their problems of energy and their problems of unemployment. And it just seems to me that this nation can cope and deal with its problems in a way that it has in the past. We're facing complex issues and problems in this nation at this time, but we have faced similar challenges at other times. And the energies and the resourcefulness of this nation, I think, should be focused on these problems in a way that brings a sense of restoration in this country by its people to—in dealing with these problems that we face—primarily the issues on the economy, the problems of inflation, and the problems of energy. And I would basically feel that—that it's imperative for this country to either move forward, that it can't stand still, or otherwise it moves back."

FEEL-GOOD QUOTE OF THE 1990S

"I want you to just let a wave of intolerance wash over you. I want you to let a wave of hatred wash over you. Yes, hate is good. . . . Our goal is a Christian nation."

Randall Terry, founder of the antiabortion group Operation Rescue, 1994.

3 THINGS THAT HAPPENED ON VICE PRESIDENT **DAN QUAYLE**'S 1989 TRIP TO THE SOUTH PACIFIC

He stopped in Hawaii and informed reporters, "Hawaii has always been a very pivotal role in the Pacific. It is in the Pacific. It is a part of the United States that is an island that is right here."

—

He stopped in American Samoa and told a group of natives, "You all look like happy campers to me. Happy campers you are, happy campers you have been and, as far as I'm concerned, happy campers you will always be."

—

He stopped in Pago Pago and called it "Pogo Pogo."

2 OBSERVATIONS ABOUT DEATH AND VICE PRESIDENTS

President **Richard Nixon** explained that he kept Vice President Spiro Agnew on the ticket in 1972 because "No assassin in his right mind would kill me."

—

Following George Bush's election in 1988, Massachusetts senator **John Kerry** said, "The Secret Service is under orders that if Bush is shot, to shoot Quayle."

5 CLASSIC UNDERSTATEMENTS

Explaining that American troops would be in Iraq for years, **George W. Bush** said, "Nobody likes war. It creates a sense of uncertainty in the country." (2006)

—

Attorney General **Ed Meese** described nuclear war as "something that may not be desirable." (1982)

President **Ronald Reagan** said of nuclear warheads, "This kind of weapon can't help but have an impact on the population as a whole." (1983)

Responding to a question about whether American lives are more important than foreign lives, Kansas senator **Bob Dole** said, "Life is very important to Americans." (1993)

Speaking of recent unfortunate events in Iraq, **George W. Bush** told reporters, "Nobody likes beheadings." (2006)

3 ASSESSMENTS BY **MICHAEL DUKAKIS** OF WHAT'S REQUIRED TO DEAL WITH THE DEFICIT

"There are only two ways to reduce the budget deficit. . . . We must do both." (April 1987)

"There are only three ways to reduce the deficit. . . . We must do all three." (September 1987)

"There are only four ways to reduce the federal budget deficit. . . . We must do all four." (August 1988)

HOW 3 WIVES FOUND OUT
THEY WERE SOON TO BE EX-WIVES

Having married his high school geometry teacher, Jackie Batt-
ley, in 1962 when he was just nineteen, freshman Georgia
representative **Newt Gingrich** was eager to be rid of her by
1980 because, as he reportedly told a friend, "She's not young
enough or pretty enough to be the wife of a president. And
besides, she has cancer." The day after she underwent her
third surgery for uterine cancer, Gingrich came to visit her,
took out a legal pad, and started discussing the terms of their
divorce. The next year he married his second wife, Marianne
Ginther, with whom he'd been committing adultery.

In 1999, Marianne Gingrich was in Ohio celebrating her
mother's eighty-fourth birthday. The phone rang and her
mother answered. It was **Newt Gingrich** calling to wish her a
happy birthday. Then he asked to talk to his wife—who had
recently been diagnosed with multiple sclerosis—and told her
that he wanted a divorce. The next year he married his third
wife, Callista Bisek, with whom he'd been committing adultery.

In 2000, New York mayor **Rudy Giuliani** held a press conference to announce his intention to separate from his wife,
Donna Hanover—a decision he'd neglected to share with her
privately.

2 INAPPROPRIATE REACTIONS TO SAD EVENTS

In the wake of the ghastly news that a woman in South Carolina had drowned her two young sons by strapping them into their car seats and rolling the car into a lake, Georgia representative **Newt Gingrich**—who stood to become Speaker of the House if enough Republicans won in the upcoming 1994 congressional elections—couldn't resist using the tragedy for political advantage. "I think the mother killing the two children in South Carolina vividly reminds every American how sick the society is getting and how much we need to change things," he said. "The only way you get change is to vote Republican."

—

Discussing the impact of the 1986 explosion of the *Challenger* space shuttle on his father's upcoming State of the Union address, **Michael Reagan** quipped, "That'll be a tough act for Dad to follow."

I MISSISSIPPI, 2 MISSISSIPPI, 3 MISSISSIPPI, 4 MISSISSIPPI

During **Haley Barbour**'s failed 1982 attempt to unseat Mississippi senator John Stennis, an aide complained that there would be "coons" at a campaign stop. Barbour warned the aide that if he continued to make racist comments, he would be reincarnated as a watermelon and placed at the mercy of blacks.

⸻

Mississippi governor **Ross Barnett**, famous for his failed 1962 effort to prevent James Meredith from enrolling in the University of Mississippi after promising that "no school will be integrated while I am your governor," opined in 1959 that "the Negro is different because God made him different to punish him."

⸻

During a heated debate about the Voting Rights Act in 1965, Mississippi senator **James O. Eastland**, who was against it, told Jewish New York senator Jacob Javits, who was for it, "I don't like you or your kind."

⸻

At a 2002 party celebrating the hundredth birthday of South Carolina senator Strom Thurmond, Mississippi senator **Trent Lott** suggested that the country would have been better off if his colleague, running as a blatant segregationist, had been elected president a half-century earlier. Lott went on a week-long apology binge that culminated in a groveling appearance on Black Entertainment Television in a failed effort to save his job as Senate majority leader. Four years later, all was forgotten and he was elected Senate minority whip.

12 WORDS WITH WHICH RICHARD NIXON GOT TO THE NUB OF THE WATERGATE PROBLEM

"The bad thing is that the president approved burglaries as a tactic." (1973)

PORTRAIT OF THE POLITICIAN AS A YOUNG MAN

During a Whittier College debate, **Richard Nixon** argued the point, "Resolved: The President Has the Inherent Power to Do What He Wants." A few years later, at Duke University Law School, he and two friends broke into the dean's office to find out their grades.

—

George W. Bush made his debut on the national stage as a Yale junior whose defense of his frat's sadistic hazing ritual of branding pledges with searing-hot wire hangers—the resulting injury left "no scarring mark physically or mentally" and was no worse than "a cigarette burn"—was picked up by the *New York Times*, thus making his first public statement an endorsement of torture.

3 REFRESHINGLY HONEST BLURTS

When a reporter observed that President Jimmy Carter didn't seem bitter about his crushing defeat in 1980 by Ronald Reagan, his wife, **Rosalynn Carter**, snapped, "I'm bitter enough for both of us."

＝

Discussing the Reagan administration's economic policies in 1981, Budget Director **David Stockman** told journalist William Greider, "None of us really understands what's going on with all these numbers."

＝

Asked during the 1980 campaign which social programs he'd cut to achieve a balanced budget, Republican presidential hopeful **George Bush** replied with startling candor, "Whatever I do will depend on whether it will help me get the nomination."

A POSSIBLE EXPLANATION FOR THE WORLD'S RAMPANT TURMOIL

In his 1991 book *The New World Order*, **Pat Robertson** asked, "How can there be peace when drunkards, drug dealers, communists, atheists, New Age worshippers of Satan, secular humanists, oppressive dictators, greedy money changers, revolutionary assassins, adulterers, and homosexuals are on top?"

SOMETHING THAT HAPPENED TO 2 CONGRESSMEN ON THE SAME DAY IN 1983

Illinois representative **Daniel Crane** was censured by the House for having an affair with a seventeen-year-old female page.

—

Massachusetts representative **Gerry Studds** was censured by the House for having an affair with a seventeen-year-old male page.

BEST EDITORIAL COMMENT ABOUT **RONALD REAGAN**'S OFT-STATED NOTION THAT TREES CAUSE MORE POLLUTION THAN CARS

The *San Jose Mercury News*: "Put the president of the Sierra Club in a sealed garage with a tree. Put **Ronald Reagan** in a sealed garage with a running automobile. Wait to see which one of them yells to get out first." (1980)

4 UNCONVINCING ARGUMENTS FOR THE CONFIRMATION OF JUDGES

Having seen his Supreme Court nominee, South Carolina judge **Clement Haynsworth**, defeated by the Senate in 1969 for, among other reasons, his history of pro-segregation decisions, President Richard Nixon—never one to take this kind of snub gracefully—told an aide to "find a good federal judge further south and further to the right." The result was Florida's undistinguished **G. Harrold Carswell**, whose past included a speech in which he'd declared, "I yield to no man . . . in the firm, vigorous belief in the principles of white supremacy, and I shall always be so governed."

Not eager to fight another battle on the race issue, Carswell's opponents focused on his utter lack of merit as a jurist, including a record as a district court judge that boasted a 58 percent reversal rate. The American Bar Association rated him merely "qualified," as opposed to the "well qualified" rating one would desire in a Supreme Court justice. With Carswell's confirmation increasingly in doubt, Nebraska senator **Roman Hruska** offered an unusual defense: "Even if he is mediocre, there are a lot of mediocre judges and people and lawyers. They are entitled to a little representation, aren't they, and a little chance? We can't have all Brandeises and Cardozos and Frankfurters and stuff like that there." This widely ridiculed observation, which, unsurprisingly, failed to save the nomination, led his obituary twenty-nine years later.

Carswell was next in the news when he was arrested in 1976 for coming on to a male vice-squad cop in a wooded area in Tallahassee.

———

Reagan appeals court nominee **Daniel Manion**—who cited among his ten "most significant" cases the defense of a client accused of improperly repairing a Volkswagen Rabbit—was confirmed by the Senate in 1986 by one vote after a red-faced, arm-waving Indiana senator **Dan Quayle** pressured Kansas senator Nancy Kassebaum into withdrawing her vote against him. On *Nightline*, Quayle told host Ted Koppel, "I'm not sure that we want all those that graduated number one or number two in their class to be on . . . our federal judiciary. This is a diversified society."

Former Indiana senator **Dan Coats** argued in favor of George W. Bush's 2005 nomination of his minimally credentialed aide **Harriet Miers** to the Supreme Court, telling CNN, "If great intellectual powerhouse is a qualification to be a member of the court and represent the American people and the wishes of the American people and to interpret the Constitution, then I think we have a court so skewed on the intellectual side that we may not be getting representation of America as a whole."

Ohio senator **Mike DeWine** also tried to make a silk purse out of the Miers sow's ear. "I think the fact she doesn't have judicial experience will add to the diversity of the Supreme Court," he said. "There is no reason everyone has to have that same background."

11 STUPEFYING MOMENTS WITH **GEORGE W. BUSH**

On his 2001 trip to London, a child asked him what the White House was like. He replied succinctly, "It is white."

While on vacation in 2002, he was about to start a round of golf when he stopped to speak to reporters about a suicide bombing that had just killed nine people in Israel. "I call upon all nations to do everything they can to stop these terrorist killings," he intoned. Then, without missing a beat, he continued, "Thank you. Now watch this drive," and teed off.

———

In an interview three months after the 9/11 attacks, summing up his first year in the White House, he said, "All in all, it's been a fabulous year for Laura and me."

———

Talking to reporters in 2001 about violence in the Middle East, he said, "The suicide bombings have increased. There's too many of them." Not a single reporter asked how many would be the right number.

———

In 2006, he campaigned for Pennsylvania representative **Don Sherwood**—an admitted adulterer who had recently settled a multi-million-dollar lawsuit in which he was accused of beating and choking his mistress—during what Bush had proclaimed as "National Character Counts Week."

———

Asked in 2004 to name his biggest mistake, he couldn't even name a small one. "I wish you'd have given me this written question ahead of time so I could plan for it," he said. "I'm sure something will pop into my head here in the midst of this press conference, with all the pressure of trying to come up with [an] answer, but it hadn't yet. . . . I don't want to sound like I have made no mistakes. I'm confident I have. I just haven't—you just put me under the spot here, and maybe I'm not as quick on my feet as I should be in coming up with one."

———

During a 2006 visit with wounded veterans from the Amputee Care Center of Brooke Army Medical Center in San Antonio, Texas, he established his solidarity with people who'd lost their limbs by saying, "As you can possibly see, I have an injury myself—not here at the hospital, but in combat with a cedar. I eventually won. The cedar gave me a little scratch."

———

Asked in 2006 what was "the best moment" during his years in the White House, he said, "I would say the best moment of all was when I caught a seven-and-a-half-pound large-mouth bass on my lake."

———

Trying to sell his Social Security reforms in 2005, he talked to a Nebraska woman who said she had three jobs. "You work three jobs?" Bush asked. "Uniquely American, isn't it? I mean, that is fantastic that you're doing that. Get any sleep?"

———

Two days after the worst attack on America in history, he said, "The most important thing is for us to find Osama bin Laden. It is our number one priority and we will not rest until we find him." Six months later to the day, with Bush frothing at the mouth to attack Saddam Hussein, a reporter asked why he rarely even mentioned the still-at-large bin Laden any more.

"You know, I just don't spend that much time on him really, to be honest with you," he replied. "I truly am not that concerned about him."

—

Standing under a MISSION ACCOMPLISHED banner on an aircraft carrier he'd just arrived on in his flight suit, he announced in May 2003, "Major combat operations in Iraq have ended. In the battle of Iraq, the United States and our allies have prevailed."

5 JOKES THAT PROBABLY SHOULD HAVE GONE UNTOLD

Agriculture Secretary **Earl Butz** lost his job in 1976 after a reporter overheard him saying, "Coloreds only want three things. You know what they want? I'll tell you what coloreds want. It's three things: first, a tight pussy; second, loose shoes; and third, a warm place to shit. That's all."

—

Arizona senator **John McCain** entertained a 1998 Republican fund-raiser by asking, "Do you know why Chelsea Clinton is so ugly? She's the child of Janet Reno and Hillary Clinton."

—

Forgetting that he was sitting in front of an open microphone, President **Ronald Reagan** warmed up for a 1984 radio address by joking, "My fellow Americans, I'm pleased to tell you today that I've signed legislation that will outlaw Russia forever. We begin bombing in five minutes."

——

Frustrated at his inability to get New York mayor Rudy Giuliani to support his candidate George Pataki for governor in 1994, New York senator **Alfonse D'Amato** told Pataki's running mate, Elizabeth McCaughey, "Betsy, come over here. I've got the way to get Giuliani on our side. You'll make him an offer he can't refuse." As so often happened with the sleazy senator, a knee-jerk denial was followed days later by a grudging apology.

——

Attempting to make fun of the ignorance of George W. Bush, Massachusetts senator **John Kerry** said in 2006, "You know, education, if you make the most of it, you study hard, you do your homework and you make an effort to be smart, you can do well." His intended punch line, "If you don't, you end up getting us stuck in a war in Iraq," got truncated to, "If you don't, you get stuck in Iraq," thus allowing desperate Republicans who were days away from losing both houses of Congress to spin this into a great insult about the intelligence of U.S. troops.

5 THINGS REV. **JERRY FALWELL** SAID THAT SHED SOME LIGHT ON WHY SO MANY PEOPLE SHED SO FEW TEARS WHEN THEY HEARD THAT HE'D DIED

"Grown men should not be having sex with prostitutes unless they are married to them."

—

"If you're not a born-again Christian, you're a failure as a human being."

—

"If he's going to be the counterfeit of Christ, [the Antichrist] has to be Jewish. The only thing we know is he must be male and Jewish."

—

"Does the law protect drug pushers? Does the law protect bootleggers? Why then should the law all of a sudden start protecting militant homosexuals who want to flaunt their perverted lifestyles in our faces?"

—

"I listen to feminists and all these radical gals, most of them are failures. They've blown it. Some of them have been married, but they married some Casper Milquetoast who asked permission to go to the bathroom. These women just need a man in the house. That's all they need. Most of the feminists need a man to tell them what time of day it is and to lead them home. And they blew it, and they're mad at all men. Feminists hate men. They're sexist. They hate men—that's their problem."

2 MISCONCEPTIONS TELEVANGELIST PAT ROBERTSON, WHO PREFERS TO BE KNOWN AS A "RELIGIOUS BROADCASTER," HAS ABOUT HOMOSEXUALITY

"I am absolutely persuaded one of the reasons so many lesbians are at the forefront of the pro-choice movement is because being a mother is the unique characteristic of womanhood, and these lesbians will never be mothers naturally, so they don't want anybody else to have that privilege either." (1993)

"[Gays] want to come into churches and disrupt church services and throw blood all around and try to give people AIDS and spit in the face of ministers." (1995)

A SILVER LINING

In 2006, *Meet the Press* host Tim Russert boldly told Secretary of State **Condoleezza Rice** that "there were a lot of misjudgments made" regarding Iraq. "There are also," she pointed out, "some misjudgments that were not made."

2 WORDS OR NOISES THAT THEIR PRONOUNCERS UNDOUBTEDLY WOULD PREFER NOT TO HAVE EMITTED

Having come in an unexpectedly disappointing third in the 2004 Iowa caucuses, presidential hopeful **Howard Dean** delivered what he himself later referred to as a "crazy, red-faced rant" in which he rattled off a litany of the upcoming states his campaign would be competing in, culminating in what instantly became known—as it was replayed literally thousands of times over the following weeks—as the "Dean Scream." Technically it was not a scream so much as a guttural noise, somewhere between a "Yeagggh!" and a "Byaah!" Whatever it was, it effectively ended his chances of being taken seriously as a presidential candidate.

———

Campaigning for re-election in 2006 while widely believed to be a front-runner for the 2008 Republican presidential nomination, Virginia senator **George Allen** self-destructed during a campaign appearance when he couldn't stop himself from referring to a young man of Indian descent (who was recording the event for Allen's opponent) as "macaca." Allen spent the rest of the campaign offering various defenses ranging from not having known what the word meant ("monkey" in French-speaking African countries like Tunisia, where Allen's mother was raised) to having concocted a series of meaningless nonsense syllables, but the damage was irreversible. His campaign went into a downward spiral wherein a reporter revealed that Allen's mother was Jewish, to which he responded that the reporter was "making aspersions" before acknowledging that it was true. Then a series of Allen's college classmates came forward to report that he'd frequently used the word "nigger"—an easily believed accusation, given his bizarre fondness for the Confederate flag, which he displayed continuously, either in his home, on his car, or on his person, from 1967 through 2000. Then, after the election, Allen was a one-term senator who nobody was talking about as a presidential candidate.

12 THINGS **GEORGE BUSH** DID DURING HIS 1988 PRESIDENTIAL CAMPAIGN

He boldly staked out pro–Pledge of Allegiance and anti-flag-burning positions.

He called for a better life for "inner ghetto city youth" and "a kitchen in every pot."

He endorsed the death penalty for drug kingpins (or, as he called them, "drugpins"), and said it was particularly appropriate "when a narcotics-wrapped-up guy goes in and murders a police officer."

He said the congressional cut-off of aid to the contras in Nicaragua "pulls the plug out from under the president of the United States."

He fairly shrieked at the Republican Convention, "Read my lips: No new taxes."

———

He declared that he stood for "anti-bigotry, anti-Semitism, anti-racism."

———

He groveled for the support of the Christian right, shamelessly gushing to Jerry Falwell, "America is in crying need of the moral vision you have brought . . . to our political life. What great goals you have!" (This prompted columnist George Will to write, "The unpleasant sound emitting from Bush as he traipses from one conservative gathering to another is a thin, tinny 'arf'—the sound of a lapdog."

———

When asked where he wanted to take the country as its president, he replied dismissively, "Oh, the vision thing."

———

He inspired a *Washington Post* editorial that called him "the Cliff Barnes of American politics—blustering, opportunistic, craven, and hopelessly ineffective all at once."

———

He got very upset during a live CBS News interview when Dan Rather dared to question him about his involvement in the Iran-contra scandal. His morning-after assessment: "I need combat pay for last night, I'll tell you. . . . You know, it's Tension City when you're in there."

===

He theorized that he finished third in an Iowa straw poll because many of his supporters were otherwise engaged "at their
daughters' coming-out parties."

===

When asked if he "recognized the equal citizenship and patrio-
tism of Americans who are atheists," he responded, "I don't
know that atheists should be considered citizens, nor should
they be considered patriots. This is one nation under God."

MOST STUNNING REVELATION

In 1969, **Richard Nixon**'s daughter **Julie Nixon Eisenhower** told
a TV interviewer that her dad was "the happiest president the
country ever had."

20 TRANSLATIONS FROM ENGLISH
TO **GEORGE W. BUSH**ESE

ENGLISH: resonate
BUSHESE: resignate, as in "doesn't seem to resignate with the
         people"

===

ENGLISH: balkanize
BUSHESE: vulcanize, as in "quotas, I think, vulcanize society"

⸻

ENGLISH: handcuffs
BUSHESE: cuff links, as in "make sure there's not this kind of federal cuff link"

⸻

ENGLISH: Greeks, Kosovars (natives of Kosovo), Timorese (natives of Timor)
BUSHESE: Grecians, Kosovians, Timorians

⸻

ENGLISH: commensurate
BUSHESE: commiserate, as in "the level commiserate with keeping the peace"

⸻

ENGLISH: ascribe
BUSHESE: subscribe, as in "you subscribe politics to it, I subscribe freedom to it"

⸻

ENGLISH: obfuscate
BUSHESE: obsfucate or obscufate

⸻

ENGLISH: tariffs and barriers
BUSHESE: terriers and bariffs, as in "if the terriers and bariffs are torn down, this economy will grow"

═

ENGLISH: tactical nuclear weapons
BUSHESE: tacular weapons

═

ENGLISH: grateful
BUSHESE: gracious, as in "I'm gracious that my brother Jeb is concerned about the hemisphere as well"

═

ENGLISH: fallibility
BUSHESE: fallacy, as in "I am a person who recognizes the fallacy of humans"

═

ENGLISH: malfeasance
BUSHESE: malfeance, as in "there was no malfeance, no attempt to hide anything"

═

ENGLISH: inalienable
BUSHESE: uninalienable, as in "they all have got uninalienable rights"

═

ENGLISH: pilloried
BUSHESE: pillared, as in "getting pillared in the press"

═

ENGLISH: subsidization
BUSHESE: subsidation, as in "Governor Bush will not stand for the subsidation of failure."

—

ENGLISH: grist
BUSHESE: gist, as in "never did it occur to me that he would become the gist for cartoonists"

—

ENGLISH: Slovenia (European country)
BUSHESE: Slovakia

—

ENGLISH: subliminal
BUSHESE: subliminable, as in "putting subliminable messages into ads"

—

ENGLISH: integral
BUSHESE: ingritable, as in "prescription drugs will be an ingritable part of the plan"

—

ENGLISH: tenets
BUSHESE: tenants, as in "I don't have to accept their tenants. I was trying to convince those college students to accept my tenants"

10 THINGS YOU MIGHT NOT KNOW ABOUT GEORGE W. BUSH'S ATTORNEY GENERAL **JOHN ASHCROFT**

While governor of Missouri, he started off a 1985 interview with an unmarried applicant for a cabinet post by asking him, "Do you have the same sexual preferences as most men?"

—

In 1998, he praised *Southern Partisan*, a virulently racist publication that defends slavery and apartheid, for helping to "set the record straight" by defending Confederate "patriots" like Robert E. Lee, Stonewall Jackson, and Jefferson Davis. Without such efforts, Ashcroft said, "we'll be taught that these people were giving their lives, subscribing their sacred fortunes and their honor to some perverted agenda," thus making it clear that he didn't consider slavery a "perverted agenda."

—

In the wake of the 9/11 attacks, 762 illegal aliens were locked up by the Justice Department and held incommunicado for months. During that time, they were denied visitors, had no access to lawyers, and were kept in solitary confinement and physically assaulted. When all was said and done, not a single one of them was linked to terrorist activities of any kind. His official response? "We make no apologies."

—

While he was willing to allow federal investigators to eavesdrop on attorney–client conversations and to spy on Web surfers virtually indiscriminately, he refused to give the FBI access to Justice Department records from gun background checks.

—

He warned those who dared to complain about post-9/11 losses of civil rights, "To those who scare peace-loving people with phantoms of lost liberty, my message is this: Your tactics only aid terrorists."

—

He liked to lighten the mood at meetings by doing his impression of Mr. Burns on *The Simpsons*.

—

Despite the urgent post-9/11 need for law enforcement officials to address terrorism issues, Ashcroft insisted on tying up ten FBI agents with the investigation of a bordello in New Orleans (where prostitution is a misdemeanor).

—

He tried to obtain the medical records of women who had partial-birth abortions to see if the procedures were really necessary.

—

He said, "It's said that we shouldn't legislate morality. Well, I think all we should legislate is morality."

—

In 2000, he lost his bid for re-election to the Senate to Missouri governor Mel Carnahan, who had died in a plane crash two weeks earlier.

LEAST HIP LEGISLATOR

Complaining about the violence in *Beavis and Butthead*, South Carolina senator **Fritz Hollings** said in 1993, "We've got this . . . what is it . . . Buffcoat and Beaver, or Beaver and something else. I haven't seen it, I don't watch it."

2 COUNTRY CLUBS

Campaigning for the 1980 presidential nomination, **Ronald Reagan** debunked the "myth" that the Republican Party was "the country club and boardroom party" in a speech delivered at a Nebraska country club.

—

Mere days after his seventeen-year-old son's 2003 arrest for aiding a beer-stealing break-in at the Burlington (VT) Country Club, presidential hopeful **Howard Dean** was asked how he intended to overcome his outsider status in the race. "The Democratic Party, all the candidates from Washington, they all know each other, they all move in the same circles, and what I'm doing is breaking into the country club," he answered, adding, "That was an incredibly unfortunate phrase."

2 FRANCOPHOBES IN THE CAN

Ohio representative **Bob Ney**, unhappy with France's 2003 refusal to support the imminent U.S. invasion of Iraq, ordered that the menus of restaurants in House office buildings replace the term "French Fries" with "Freedom Fries," and that "French Toast" henceforth be known as "Freedom Toast." Four years later, having resigned from Congress and pleaded guilty to charges connected to the Jack Abramoff bribery scandal, Ney's freedom was replaced with a thirty-month prison sentence.

California representative **Randy "Duke" Cunningham**, similarly displeased with the French, struck a blow for freedom by announcing, "I took the Grey Poupon out of my cupboard." Three years later, having resigned from Congress and pleaded guilty to tax evasion, bribery, and various frauds, he began serving a 100-month prison sentence.

RICHARD NIXON MAKES EXCUSES FOR A DRUG ADDICT (BUT NOT JUST ANY DRUG ADDICT)

On tape at his presidential library, Richard Nixon discussed his 1970 White House encounter with Elvis Presley, the iconic photo of which showed "the King" to be totally stoned. "Well, he was very flamboyant," Nixon said. "My daughters knew him and heard him. I didn't know that much about him except what I read. But as I talked to him, I sensed that basically he's a very shy man. Flamboyancy was covering up the shyness. He was also a very sincere man," continued Nixon, whose bizarre affinity for Presley might be attributed to the fact that their birthdays were a day apart (January 8th for Elvis, the 9th for Dick). "He wanted to be an example to young people. And people say that because, later on, it was found that he had used drugs, that therefore he could not be a good example. They overlooked the fact that he never used illegal drugs. It was always drugs prescribed by his physican. But I think he was a very decent man."

THE TRULY GREAT THING ABOUT THE NIXON/PRESLEY CONFAB

Nixon thought he could use Presley in his antidrug efforts. "I think you can reach young people in a way no one in the government can," he said, and Elvis quickly agreed. "I can go right into a group of hippies and young people and be accepted," he said. "This can be real helpful." Then, having buttered Nixon up, Presley got to his own agenda: "Mr. President, can you get me a badge from the Narcotics Bureau? I've been trying to get a badge from them for my collection." Nixon told an aide, "I'd like to do that. See that he gets one," prompting an excited Elvis to surprise him with a big hug. But then, Presley had a right to be joyous—the federal drug agent's badge he'd tricked Tricky Dick into giving him protected him from then on from any airport searches.

2 INTERESTING POLLS

In a 2005 Pew Research Center poll asking respondents for the first word that came into their mind when they thought about **George W. Bush**, "incompetent" came in first, "idiot" was third, and "liar" fourth. "Ass" was tenth.

In an Associated Press/Ipsos poll asking Americans to pick the "biggest villain" of 2006, more people (25 percent) picked **George W. Bush** than the next four choices (Osama bin Laden, Saddam Hussein, Mahmoud Ahmadinejad, and Kim Jong Il) combined.

2 PROFILES IN LACK OF COURAGE

Despite his serious skepticism about the veracity of the intelligence claiming that Iraq possessed weapons of mass destruction, Secretary of State **Colin Powell**, whose resignation in protest might well have prevented the Iraq War, instead chose to help build the case for the U.S. invasion by telling a 2003 session of the United Nations Security Council that "there can be no doubt that Saddam Hussein has biological weapons," and that "there is no doubt in my mind" that he was seeking components for nuclear weapons.

After referring to a 2006 bill loosening restrictions on the use of tactics commonly thought of as torture and stripping anyone deemed an "enemy combatant" of the right of habeus corpus as "patently unconstitutional on its face," Pennsylvania senator **Arlen Specter** voted for it.

A PROFILE IN SELFISHNESS

Given that the party breakdown in the Senate after the 2000 election was tied 50–50, **Joe Lieberman**'s insistence on running for both his Senate seat and the vice presidency in 2000, in retrospect, insured a Republican-controlled Senate, regardless of the results of either race. Obviously, his not becoming vice president made Dick Cheney the tie-breaking vote in the Senate, thus giving Republicans control, but even if the Supreme Court hadn't overridden the election results, Lieberman's Senate seat would then have been vacated, with his replacement being named by the governor of Connecticut—a Republican.

CHERTOFF TO CITY: DROP DEAD

Homeland Security chief **Michael Chertoff** cut $83 million from New York's 2006 antiterrorism funds because he said the city—home of the Empire State Building, the United Nations, the Statue of Liberty, the Brooklyn Bridge, the Stock Exchange, and Rockefeller Center—had no national monuments or icons that could be considered terrorist targets.

GET OUT OF JAIL FREE

Marc Rich, an international financier indicted in 1983 in what was the largest tax-evasion case in U.S. history up to that point, was pardoned by President **Bill Clinton** in 2001, despite his never having returned to the country to face charges. His wife, Denise, was a major Democratic contributor and Clinton Library benefactor.

━━

Caspar Weinberger, Elliott Abrams, Robert McFarlane, and three other Iran-contra convictees were pardoned in 1992 by President **George Bush**, whose involvement in that scandal remained mysterious. Of course, any of these men might have shed some light on that involvement if, say, they hadn't been pardoned.

━━

Dick Cheney's chief of staff **I. Lewis "Scooter" Libby** had his thirty-month sentence for obstruction of justice and perjury in connection with the revenge outing of covert CIA operative Valerie Plame commuted by **George W. Bush** in 2007.

━━

One month into his presidency, **Gerald Ford** pardoned **Richard Nixon**, thus depriving the nation of what would surely have been the trial of the millennium.

MOST OUT-THERE PARAGRAPH
BY AN INCREASINGLY EMACIATED
HORSE-FACED HARRIDAN

In her 2006 book *Godless*, **Ann Coulter** went after the high-profile 9/11 widows known as the Jersey Girls, whose demands for an investigation into the intelligence and security failures that allowed the attacks obviously stuck in her craw. "These broads are millionaires, lionized on TV and in articles about them, reveling in their status as celebrities and stalked by grief-arrazies. I've never seen people enjoying their husband's death so much," she wrote. "And by the way, how do we know their husbands weren't planning to divorce these harpies? Now that their shelf life is dwindling, they'd better hurry up and appear in *Playboy*."

LEAST LIKELY BOOK FOR SOMEONE
RESPONSIBLE FOR THE FATE OF THE
NATION TO BE UNABLE TO PUT DOWN
IN A MOMENT OF ULTIMATE CRISIS

After being notified of the second plane crashing into the World Trade Center while reading *My Pet Goat* to a classroom of Florida preschoolers, **George W. Bush** did not leap out of his seat, make his excuses, and rush out of the room, but rather continued to sit there with the book in his hands for seven more minutes, until an aide finally suggested that maybe he had something more important to do.

3 THOUGHTS ABOUT
SAME-SEX MARRIAGE

An advance copy of a 2004 speech by Texas senator **John Cornyn** supporting a Constitutional amendment forbidding gay marriage contained this thought: "It does not affect your daily life very much if your neighbor marries a box turtle. But that does not mean it is right. Now you must raise your children up in a world where that union of man and box turtle is on the same legal footing as man and wife." Though he wisely chose not to actually say these words, the quote was too good not to become known.

Campaigning for the governorship of California in 2003, **Arnold Schwarzenegger** declared, "Gay marriage should be between a man and a woman."

Supporting an anti-same-sex-marriage amendment, Louisiana senator **David Vitter** said in 2006, "I don't think there's any issue that's more important than this one," defining himself as "a conservative who opposes radically redefining marriage, the most important social institution in human history." So, when his number turned up the next year in the phone records of the "D.C. Madam," many folks were amused.

3 UNLIKELY STORIES

President **Ronald Reagan** claimed that a never-named blind supporter "wrote in Braille to tell me that if cutting his pension would help get this country back on its feet, he'd like to have me cut his pension."

＝

In 1991, Virginia senator **Chuck Robb**—married to Lyndon Johnson's daughter Lynda—admitted having been alone in a hotel room in 1984, while he was governor, with beauty contest winner Tai Collins, though he insisted that things progressed no further than them drinking champagne and her giving him a nude massage. According to her, they'd had a lengthy affair.

＝

Testifying to the Senate ethics committee in 1988 about the worthiness of Charles Keating, inadvertent architect of a tsunami of savings and loan association collapses in the late 1980s, Arizona senator **Dennis DeConcini** said, "When I met Mother Teresa, I believe it was in 1986 in this city, and I was introduced to her and told her what state I came from. And the first thing she said to me was, 'How is my friend, Charlie Keating?'"

TOUGH-GUY TALK THAT EVOKED
GIGGLES RATHER THAN RESPECT

"We cannot let terrorists and rogue nations hold this nation hostile, or hold our allies hostile."
   George W. Bush, 2000.

"[The terrorists] will not hold America blackmail."
   George W. Bush, 2002.

"There's no cave deep enough for America, or dark enough to hide."
   George W. Bush, 2002.

4 VIVID METAPHORS

Former secretary of the treasury **Paul O'Neill**, as quoted by Ron Suskind in his 2004 book, *The Price of Loyalty: George W. Bush, the White House, and the Education of Paul O'Neill:* "[George W. Bush at a Cabinet meeting is like] a blind man in a roomful of deaf people. There is no discernable connection."

Antitax fanatic **Grover Norquist** in 2001: "I don't want to abolish government. I simply want to reduce it to the size where I can drag it into the bathroom and drown it in the bathtub."

Describing his under-the-radar efforts to get sympathetic voters to the polls and defeat more secular candidates, Christian Coalition executive director **Ralph Reed** said in 1991, "I want to be invisible. I do guerrilla warfare. I paint my face and travel at night. You don't know it's over until you're in a body bag."

Opining that President Ronald Reagan would have to fire some people in connection with the 1986 Iran-contra arms-for-hostages scandal, **John Ehrlichman**—who, on the Watergate tapes, was heard suggesting that acting FBI head L. Patrick Gray be left to "twist slowly, slowly in the wind"—said, "He's got to throw some of those babies out of the sleigh."

2 RENOWNED REGURGITATORS

In 1985, Utah senator **Jake Garn**, the first legislator in space, joined the crew of the space shuttle *Discovery*, where his participation in motion-sickness experiments earned him the sobriquet "Barfin' Jake."

At a 1992 state dinner in Tokyo, a flu-ridden President **George Bush** keeled over after vomiting on the Japanese prime minister. His spokesman, Marlin Fitzwater, got a beeper message: "President barfed."

8 THINGS VICE PRESIDENT DAN QUAYLE DID DURING HIS SECOND YEAR IN OFFICE

He stopped at a coastal village in Chile to buy souvenirs and chose an American Indian doll with an enormous erection, telling his wife, "This is something teenage boys might find of interest."

He addressed a group of Arizona Republicans and told them, "If we do not succeed, then we run the risk of failure."

He gave a speech to NASA employees and told them, "For NASA, space is still a high priority."

He delivered a speech about education in which he observed, "Quite frankly, teachers are the only profession that teach our children."

He said of the always volatile situation in the Middle East, "We are ready for any unforeseen event that may or may not occur."

He announced his support for efforts "to limit the terms of members of Congress, especially members of the House and members of the Senate."

———

He apologized for golfing at a country club that excludes blacks, but said he would continue to play at a course that excludes women.

———

With a U.S. invasion of Iraq looming, he explained that fears of the conflict becoming another Vietnam were groundless because "Vietnam is a jungle. You had jungle warfare. Kuwait, Iraq, Saudi Arabia, you have sand." He added that another reason not to fear a protracted war was that "from an historical basis, Middle East conflicts do not last a long time."

2 GRATUITOUS INSULTS TO THE ASIAN COMMUNITY

In the midst of the 1995 O. J. Simpson murder trial, New York senator **Alfonse D'Amato** went on *Imus in the Morning* and made fun of Judge Lance Ito by speaking in a Jerry Lewis–type Japanese accent. Though there were many aspects of Ito's performance worthy of mockery, his accent-free American speaking style was not one of them.

———

Pat Robertson said that plastic surgery addicts "got the eyes like they're Oriental." Lest the meaning of this 2007 observation not be clear, he stretched his eyes back to avoid any misunderstanding.

8 THINGS **GEORGE W. BUSH**
THINKS ARE IMPORTANT

"Home is important. It's important to have a home." (2001)

—

"[Africa is] an important continent." (2000)

—

"I've been elected governor twice in an incredibly important state." (1999)

—

"The important question is, How many hands have I shaked?" (1999)

—

"It's important for us to explain to our nation that life is important. It's not only the life of babies, but it's life of children living in, you know, the dark dungeons of the Internet." (2000)

—

"I think it's important for those of us in a position of responsibility to be firm in sharing our experiences, to understand that the babies out of wedlock is a very difficult chore for mom and baby alike. . . . And, you know, hopefully, condoms will work, but it hasn't worked." (1999)

—

"It's very important for folks to understand that when there's more trade, there's more commerce." (2001)

‗

"The thing that's important for me is to remember what's the most important thing." (2001)

3 PISS-POOR MEMORIES

National Security Advisor **John Poindexter** used the phrase "I can't recall," or some variation of it, almost two hundred times during his 1987 Iran-contra testimony.

‗

Attorney General **Ed Meese** used the phrase "I don't recall," or some variation of it, over three hundred times during his 1987 Iran-contra testimony.

‗

Attorney General **Alberto Gonzales** used the phrase "I don't recall," or some variation of it, more than seventy times in 2007 during Senate questioning about the political firing of eight U.S. attorneys.

10 DEFINING DEBATE MOMENTS

Doubtlessly believing that makeup was for sissies, Vice President **Richard Nixon** refused to wear any for his first presidential debate with Massachusetts senator John F. Kennedy, resulting in an unfortunate display of five o'clock shadow that made him look, in the words of one sadly anonymous observer, "like a sinister chipmunk." Though Nixon was perceived to have won the debate by those who listened to it on the radio, his shifty appearance dissuaded enough television viewers from voting for him to cost him the very close 1960 election.

———

When the sound suddenly went dead during their first debate in 1976, President **Gerald Ford** and **Jimmy Carter** stood silently for almost half an hour, with neither man uttering a sound, moving an inch from his podium, or acknowledging the other in any way.

———

During the second Ford–Carter debate, President **Gerald Ford** made the surprising claim that "there is no Soviet domination of Eastern Europe and there never will be under a Ford administration," adding that he didn't believe that Yugoslavians, Romanians, or Poles considered themselves so dominated. He stubbornly refused to admit his error for several days, thus allowing the headlines a month before the election to be dominated by the story of his ignorance.

———

The first-ever vice presidential debate, between Ford's running mate, Kansas senator **Bob Dole**, and Carter's running mate, Minnesota senator Walter Mondale, featured Dole's observation that Democrats had been in office during the start of all four twentieth-century wars the U.S. was involved in, and that the number of American casualties in those "Democrat wars" was about the same as the population of Detroit. Dole's decision to present himself to a country numbed by Watergate as a scowling Nixonian figure was, to say the least, peculiar.

━━

In the middle of his single 1980 debate with Ronald Reagan, President **Jimmy Carter** attempted to get in the last word on the subject of an arms limitation treaty by saying, "I had a discussion with my daughter Amy the other day before I came here to ask me [*sic*] what the most important issue was. She said she thought nuclear weaponry and the control of nuclear arms." This effort to evoke warmth and fuzziness in the audience instead inspired contempt, as the more common reaction was not, "Aww, what a sweet dad," but rather, "What the hell is the president doing asking a thirteen-year-old what's important?" That moment, combined with Reagan's avuncular, well-rehearsed "There you go again" rejoinder to Carter's bringing up Reagan's opposition to national health insurance—something the Reagan team was waiting for, as they'd stolen copies of Carter's debate briefing books—sealed his fate as a one-term president.

━━

In his first 1984 debate with Walter Mondale, president and former actor **Ronald Reagan** explained that a considerable portion of the defense budget was spent on "food and wardrobe," thus becoming the first president to refer to military uniforms in this way. Though this and many other things he said or couldn't think of the words to say suddenly made viewers question his all-thereness, his perfect delivery of a well-rehearsed one-liner in the second debate—"I will not make age an issue in this campaign. I am not going to exploit for political purposes my opponent's youth and inexperience"—made more than enough voters forget that two weeks earlier he'd seemed like a senile old fool.

—

Drowning in ridicule following his selection as George Bush's running mate, Indiana senator **Dan Quayle** was determined to use his 1988 encounter with his Democratic counterpart, Texas senator Lloyd Bentsen, to demonstrate the true depth of his qualifications, among them that he knew British Prime Minister Margaret Thatcher and German President Helmut Kohl and "they know me." Asked three times what he would actually do if he suddenly became president, he three times responded by robotically reciting his meager credentials, adding defiantly, "I have as much experience in the Congress as Jack Kennedy did when he sought the presidency." Bentsen, with all the gravity so obviously lacking in his opponent, replied somberly, "Senator, I served with Jack Kennedy. I knew Jack Kennedy. Jack Kennedy was a friend of mine. Senator, you're no Jack Kennedy." If there was a chart for most frequently broadcast soundbites, that one would surely be in the all-time top ten.

—

Unaware that he would be participating in a debate with Vice President Dan Quayle and Tennessee senator Al Gore until a week before the 1992 event, H. Ross Perot's running mate, Vice Admiral **James Stockdale**, attempted to introduce himself to the nation with his opening statement, "Who am I? Why am I here?" As Stockdale was completely inexperienced in public debating, he mistakenly thought that he'd be given time to answer those questions and tell Americans who he was—among other things, a prisoner of war for seven years in Vietnam and one of the most decorated officers in navy history. Instead, his words were interpreted as the befuddled ramblings of a confused old man, which was the portrait of him instantly etched in the national consciousness.

⸺

During his second 1992 debate with Bill Clinton, President **George Bush** was so eager for it to end that he kept checking his watch—a move repeatedly caught on camera.

⸺

With expectations for **George W. Bush**'s performance in the first 2000 presidential debate so low that even an outburst of Tourette's might not have qualified as "worse than expected," **Al Gore**'s inability to stop sighing contemptuously—albeit deservedly—at Bush's answers, combined with his incessant repetition of the word "lockbox," created the perception that Bush had won.

LEAST HELPFUL OBSERVATION

On the occasion of his 2004 resignation as secretary of Health and Human Services, **Tommy Thompson** marveled, "For the life of me, I cannot understand why the terrorists have not attacked our food supply, because it is so easy to do."

2 QUICK CASH-INS

Fifteen months after his defeat in the 1976 election, **Gerald Ford** became the first former president to "sell out" and get paid for endorsing a product, in this case a 100-medal Franklin Mint series of key events in the American presidency.

Three months after her defeat in the 1984 election, vice presidential candidate **Geraldine Ferraro** signed on to appear in ads for Diet Pepsi.

UNLIKELIEST SOURCE OF PRIDE

Oklahoma senator **James Inhofe** boasted in 2007, "I have been called—my kids are aware of this—dumb, crazy man, science abuser, Holocaust denier, villain of the month, hate-filled, warmonger, Neanderthal, Genghis Khan, and Attila the Hun. And I can just tell you that I wear some of those titles proudly."

LEAST AUSPICIOUS CAMPAIGN KICKOFF

Unofficially announcing his entry into the 2008 presidential race, Delaware senator **Joe Biden** said on *Meet the Press* in 2007, "I'm going to be Joe Biden, and I'm going to try to be the best Biden I can be. If I can, I have a shot. If I can't, I lose."

Unfortunately, being Joe Biden meant talking without thinking, so he spent the day of his official announcement a few weeks later explaining his condescending comments about Barack Obama ("I mean, you got the first mainstream African-American who is articulate and bright and clean and a nice-looking guy. I mean, that's a storybook, man") that appeared that morning in an article in the *New York Observer*.

THE PLUSES AND MINUSES OF MEN AND WOMEN IN THE MILITARY, ACCORDING TO **NEWT GINGRICH** (WHO DIDN'T SERVE)

"If you talk about being in combat, what does combat mean? If combat means being in a ditch, females have biological problems staying in a ditch for thirty days because they get infections, and they don't have upper body strength. I mean, some do, but they're relatively rare. On the other hand, men are basically little piglets. You drop them in the ditch, they roll around in it, doesn't matter, you know. These things are very real. On the other hand, if combat means being on an Aegis class cruiser managing the computer controls for twelve ships and their rockets, a female again may be dramatically better than a male who gets very, very frustrated sitting in a chair all the time because males are biologically driven to go out and hunt giraffes." (1995)

10 ESPECIALLY ENTERTAINING
GEORGE W. BUSH LANGUAGE MANGLINGS

"That day when they swear us in, when I put my hand on the Bible, I will swear to not—to uphold the laws of the land." (2000)

—

"We'll be tough and resolute as we unite, to make sure freedom stands, to rout out evil, to say to our children and grandchildren, we were bold enough to act, without tiring, so that you can live in a great land and in a peaceful world. And there's no doubt in my mind, not one doubt in my mind, that we will fail." (2001)

—

"Republicans and Democrats stood with me in the Rose Garden to announce their support for a clear statement of purpose [to Saddam Hussein]: You disarm or we will." (2002)

—

"We've got to have an education system that is next to none." (2002)

—

"We need an energy bill that encourages consumption." (2002)

—

"Our enemies are innovative and resourceful, and so are we. They never stop thinking about new ways to harm our country and our people, and neither do we." (2004)

—

"That's why I went to the Congress last September and proposed fundamental—supplemental funding, which is money for armor and body parts and ammunition and fuel." (2004)

—

"You know, one of the hardest parts of my job is to connect Iraq to the war on terror." (2006)

—

"And there is distrust in Washington. I am surprised, frankly, at the amount of distrust that exists in this town. And I'm sorry it's the case, and I'll work hard to try to elevate it." (2007)

—

"One of my concerns is that the health care not be as good as it can possibly be." (2007)

2 SERIOUS UNDERESTIMATIONS OF PUBLIC MEMORY

Explaining his decision not to visit a concentration camp on his 1985 excursion to a Nazi cemetery at Bitburg, President **Ronald Reagan** claimed that there were very few living Germans who even remembered World War II, "and certainly none of them who were adults and participating in any way." At the time, young men of army age in the early 1940s would have been in their sixties.

Former Nixon speechwriter **Ben Stein** wrote a 1984 *Washington Post* op-ed column on the tenth anniversary of the first presidential resignation in which he asked, "Really, who now knows what Watergate was about? What was all the shouting about? If whatever Nixon did was so obscure that no one can even remember what he did any longer . . . how drastic could it have been? . . . If the nation chased a President out of office for the only time in 200 years *and no one clearly remembers why*, something went drastically wrong." Answering him in an editorial, the paper said, "Not to put too fine a point on it, we think we can remember."

6 TAPED CONVERSATIONS THAT MIGHT LEAD ONE TO BELIEVE **RICHARD NIXON**'S OVAL OFFICE WAS THE BACK ROOM OF THE BADA BING CLUB

During a 1971 discussion about how to break up demonstrations against the Vietnam War, White House Chief of Staff **H. R. Haldeman** suggested using Teamsters Union "thugs" to attack the protesters.

"They, they've got guys who'll go in and knock their heads off," President Nixon chuckled.

"Sure," Haldeman replied. "Murderers. Guys that really, you know, that's what they really do. . . . They're gonna beat the shit out of some of these people. And, uh, and hope they really hurt 'em. You know, I mean go in . . . and smash some noses."

——

Upset with critical television coverage of the Vietnam War, President Nixon told Attorney General **John Mitchell** in 1971, "We have to screw the networks. They've got to be screwed. They're terrible people. They're a bunch of bastards."

Then, to be sure he'd made his point, the president added, "I want you to screw them and screw them good."

——

With two months to go until the 1972 election, President Nixon was already salivating at the post-election prospect of making his opponents' lives miserable by auditing their tax returns. To avoid the perception that this would be a vendetta against Democrats, Chief of Staff **H. R. Haldeman** suggested, "We'll pull a lot of Republicans, too, and just don't look at those after we pull 'em."

"We've got to do it," the president said, "even if we've got to kick [IRS Commissioner Johnnie M.] Walters's ass out first and get a man in there."

And what kind of guy did President Nixon want as commissioner of the Internal Revenue Service? "I want to be sure that he is a ruthless son of a bitch, that he will do what he's told, that every income tax return I want to see, I see. That he will go after our enemies and not go after our friends. Now, it's as simple as that. If he isn't, he doesn't get the job."

And why was it, he wondered, that his opponent George McGovern's income tax files had not been investigated? "There are so many damn Democrats [at the IRS]," his counsel **John Dean** said. "It would have to be an artful job to go down and get that file."

"There are ways to do that," said the president. "God damn it, sneak in in the middle of the night."

—

Speaking to his soon-to-be attorney general Richard Kleindienst in 1972 about creating an opportunity to name yet another conservative to the Supreme Court, President Nixon asked, "Who are you going to shoot?"

—

Two months before the 1972 election, President Nixon ordered that a spy—"one that can cover him around the clock, every place he goes"—be planted in the Secret Service detail he had ordered for Sen. Edward Kennedy in the wake of the assassination attempt on George Wallace.

"We might just get lucky and catch this son of a bitch [committing adultery]," the president gloated. "Ruin him for '76. It's going to be fun."

—

President Nixon believed that there were documents in the liberal Brookings Institute think tank that could be used to "blackmail [former president Lyndon] Johnson." A year to the day before the Watergate break-in, he had an idea about how to get them.

"Goddamn it, get in and get those files," the president told **H. R. Haldeman**. "Blow the safe and get them."

As often happened with such orders, the president's underlings did nothing, hoping he would forget about them, but he kept bringing it up.

"The way I want that handled," he said on another occasion, "is . . . just to break in. Break in and take it out! You understand? . . . You are to break into the place, rifle the files, and bring them out."

"I don't have any problem breaking in," Haldeman said.

"Just go in and take it!" the president said. "Go in around eight or nine o'clock. And clean it up."

In another meeting, the attorney general's reservations came up. "Mitchell was arguing strenuously about the law this morning," said the president, "and I said, 'Goddamn it, forget the law.'"

President Nixon continued to refine his plan over the next several days, adding a firebombing that would allow FBI agents to accompany firemen into the building and steal the desired documents, but ultimately nothing happened.

A GLARING INSTANCE OF
MISPLACED INDIGNATION

As the Watergate scandal continued to metastasize, **President Nixon** met with Bob Dole, the former chairman of the Republican National Committee. "They have people accusing the president of everything from thievery to cover-up to lying," Nixon huffed. "Jesus Christ."

11 BOLD DECLARATIONS OF THE OBVIOUS

Before his first presidential debate against Al Gore in 2000, **George W. Bush** declared, "I view this as a chance for people to get an impression of me on a stage debating my opponent."

—

In 1988, vice presidential candidate **Dan Quayle** told NBC's Tom Brokaw, "A family is very important, particularly to the children."

—

At a 1992 luncheon with *Washington Times* editors and reporters, Virginia governor **Douglas Wilder** pronounced, "The first black president will be a politician who is black."

—

After his 2001 meeting with Vladimir Putin, **George W. Bush** reported that he'd told the Russian president, "It's negative to think about blowing each other up. That's not a positive thought."

—

During his 1980 presidential debate with the independent candidate, Illinois representative John Anderson, **Ronald Reagan** declared, "I notice that everybody who's for abortion has already been born."

—

In 1988, vice presidential candidate **Dan Quayle** informed Ohio high school students that Israel is "very important to the U.S." and that AIDS is "a very serious disease."

‗

Speaking in Tucson in 2005, **George W. Bush** observed, "Those who enter the country illegally violate the law."

‗

Campaigning in Ohio two weeks before the 1988 election, presidential candidate **George Bush** told a crowd, "It's no exaggeration to say that the undecideds could go one way or another and determine the election."

‗

Following the 2001 overflowing of the Mississippi River into the streets of Prairie du Chen, Wisconsin, governor **Scott McCallum** pointed out, "There's a lot of stress involved after your house is underwater."

‗

Acknowledging that "the Iraq War has created a sense of consternation here in America," **George W. Bush** told reporters at a 2006 press conference, "I mean, when you turn on your TV screen and see innocent people die, day in and day out, it affects the mentality of our country."

5 GUYS WHO COULDN'T KEEP
THEIR HANDS TO THEMSELVES

Washington senator **Brock Adams** decided not to seek reelection in 1992 after at least nine women accused him of various forms of sexual transgressions over two decades, ranging from surreptitious breast, thigh, and buttock fondling to drugging and rape.

━━

The book *Women on the Hill* by Clara Bingham recounted a 1994 incident in which South Carolina senator **Strom Thurmond** encountered Washington senator Patty Murray on an elevator, "put his arm around her, groping for her breast, and said in a deep Carolina drawl, 'Are you married, little lady?'" Thurmond was ninety-one at the time.

━━

After twenty-six years in the Senate, Oregon's serial groper **Bob Packwood** resigned his seat in 1995 after more than two dozen women claimed to have been the subjects of his unwanted sexual advances.

━━

A 2003 *Los Angeles Times* article collected the allegations of six women who recounted vulgar gropings by **Arnold Schwarzenegger** over the previous three decades. Despite the article's itemizing of the various offenses and where they took place (a gym, a street, a hotel room, an office, an elevator, and a restaurant), Schwarzenegger's apology was crafted to fool the public into believing that the incidents could all be chalked up to overexuberant behavior on "rowdy movie sets," and the public was so fooled, as he was elected governor a month later.

━━

While President **Bill Clinton** was defending himself against a sexual harassment lawsuit by Paula Jones, two more women—

Kathleen Willey and Juanita Broderick—came forward to say that they'd been sexually assaulted by him. As neither of them had any proof, and indeed had both previously denied that such events took place, they were not taken seriously by a country already sick to death of thinking about Bill Clinton's sex life.

2 HYPOTHETICAL QUESTIONS

During a 1984 Democratic primary debate, Colorado senator **Gary Hart** was asked by moderator John Chancellor what he would do if, as president, he received a report that a Czechoslovak plane full of people was flying toward U.S. Strategic Air Command bases and ignoring U.S. warnings to turn back. "If the people they looked in and saw had uniforms on, I would shoot the aircraft down," he said. "If they were civilians, I would just let them keep going." The absurdity of this answer was quickly pointed out by Ohio senator John Glenn, a former astronaut and jet fighter pilot, who observed with a chuckle, "You don't go peeking in the windows to see if they have uniforms on."

———

The second 1988 presidential debate started with moderator Bernard Shaw asking **Michael Dukakis**, "If Kitty Dukakis were raped and murdered, would you favor an irrevocable death penalty for the killer?" Instead of having a normal human reaction—for example, outrage at Shaw for conjuring up such a hideous scenario—Dukakis answered like one of the pod people in *Invasion of the Body Snatchers*, droning out an emotionless response about how there's no evidence that capital punishment is a deterrent. And with that, any chance of a Dukakis presidency was crushed like a bug.

2 THINGS **DONALD RUMSFELD** SAID WE KNOW FOR SURE ABOUT OSAMA BIN LADEN

"We do know of certain knowledge that he is either in Afghanistan, or in some other country, or dead." (2001)

—

"He is either alive and well or alive and not too well or not alive." (2002)

10 WALLOWS IN SCHADENFREUDE

In the midst of the run-up to the 1998 impeachment of Bill Clinton, Indiana representative **Dan Burton**, one of the most rabid champions of said impeachment—"This guy's a scumbag, that's why I'm after him," he explained—was forced to admit that he had a fifteen-year-old illegitimate son.

—

Days after the Burton revelation, Idaho representative **Helen Chenoweth**, who'd been running a TV ad stating that "per-

sonal conduct does count" to attack Bill Clinton for his dalli-
ance with Monica Lewinsky, was forced to admit that she'd had
a long affair in the 1980s with a married man. Still, she wanted
to be sure it was understood that, unlike the president's, her
indiscretions occurred "when I was a private citizen and a
single woman."

Days after the Chenoweth revelation, Illinois representative
Henry Hyde, head of the House Judiciary Committee that was
preparing impeachment proceedings against Bill Clinton, was
forced to admit that he'd had a four-year affair three decades
earlier. Hyde referred to his infidelity as one of his "youthful indiscretions," though he'd been in his early forties at the time.

Two days before the House impeached Bill Clinton, Speaker-
elect **Bob Livingston** was forced to admit that he had "on occasion strayed" during his thirty-three-year marriage, though he
took pains to point out that his infidelities did not involve youthful interns or perjury. He stepped down as Speaker-elect and
announced his imminent resignation from Congress hours before the impeachment vote was taken.

While Rev. **Jesse Jackson** was advising Bill Clinton how to survive the Lewinsky scandal, his mistress was pregnant with his
illegitimate daughter.

Republican presidential candidate **Pat Robertson** admitted in 1987 that his first child was born a mere ten weeks after his marriage, complaining, "I have never had this kind of precision demanded of me before."

———

In 1982, rabid right-winger **John G. Schmitz** admitted having fathered two illegitimate children. Fifteen years later, as an added bonus, he was revealed to be the father of statutory rapist Mary Kay Letourneau.

———

Moral scold **William Bennett** admitted in 2003 to a multi-million-dollar gambling habit, with a particular weakness for one-armed bandits. Denying that he was a hypocrite, Bennett explained, "I never got on the soapbox about gambling. I never said, 'You know, gambling is a terrible thing, people should stop gambling.'"

———

Right-wing talk show host **Rush Limbaugh**, whose on-air rants frequently attacked illegal drug users and advocated their imprisonment, admitted in 2003 that he was addicted to OxyContin.

———

White House shill **James Guckert**, who was given daily press passes under his pseudonym Jeff Gannon despite never having had an article published and not being affiliated with any reputable journalistic enterprise, attracted too much attention at a 2005 press conference when he asked George W. Bush how he expected to work with Senate Democrats, whom he described as "people who seem to have divorced themselves from reality." The investigation into his background that was prompted by this obvious partisanship led to the revelation that there were naked pictures of him on the Internet, specifically on several gay escort sites.

ANGRIEST REACTION TO BEING LURED TO A HOTEL ROOM BY A SUPPOSED GIRLFRIEND AND BEING BURST IN ON BY THE FBI AFTER BEING VIDEOTAPED SUCKING ON A CRACK PIPE

"Bitch set me up. . . . This goddamn bitch, setting me up like this. Set me up, ain't that a bitch . . . goddamn bitch."

Washington, D.C., mayor **Marion Barry** in 1990, who subsequently offered as an excuse, "I have spent so much time caring about and worrying about and doing for others, I have not worried about or cared enough for myself."

THE 4 MOST FAMOUS INSULTS HURLED BY VICE PRESIDENT **SPIRO AGNEW** AT THE "RADICAL LIBERALS"—OR, IN AGNEWESE, "RADIC-LIBS"—WHO ULTIMATELY HAD THE LAST LAUGH WHEN HE HAD TO RESIGN HIS OFFICE TO STAY OUT OF JAIL

"Nattering nabobs of negativism."

—

"Hopeless, hysterical hypochondriacs of history."

—

"Pusillanimous pussyfooters." (Alternately, "Pusillanimous purveyors of permissiveness.")

—

"An effete corps of impudent snobs who characterize themselves as intellectuals."

THE CLASSIC **SPIRO AGNEW** QUOTE THAT DESERVEDLY MADE IT INTO *BARTLETT'S*

"I've been in many of them and to some extent I would have to say this: if you've seen one city slum you've seen them all." (1968)

3 LIES **GEORGE W. BUSH** TOLD ABOUT ENRON IN 2002

He claimed that Enron chairman Kenneth Lay "was a supporter of Ann Richards" in the 1994 Texas gubernatorial race, though Lay actually gave many times more money to Bush and even declared for him.

—

He implied that Lay was a Richards administration holdover that he first "got to know" after being elected governor, though they'd actually worked together on the 1992 Republican convention.

—

He expressed outrage that his own mother-in-law bought $8,000 worth of Enron stock "last summer," though she actually purchased it in 1999.

2 FOLKS WHO THOUGHT TOO MUCH WAS MADE OF THE WHOLE ENRON THING

"Companies come and go. It's part of the genius of capitalism."
Secretary of the Treasury **Paul O'Neill**.

—

"They act like there's some billing records, or some cattle scam, or some fired travel aides, or some blue dress."

Cheney aide **Mary Matalin**, complaining with the usual sneer in her voice about the chutzpah of the press to be covering the Enron scandal, in which thousands of people lost their life savings and retirement funds, as if it was as important as some hyped-up nonscandal or someone lying about a blow job.

2 TANTRUMS

When Israeli Prime Minister Yitzhak Rabin was assassinated in 1995, President Bill Clinton took a large delegation to Israel on *Air Force One* for the funeral. After returning home, House Speaker **Newt Gingrich**'s spokesman Tony Blankley sent Clinton's spokesman Mike McCurry a letter (simultaneously leaked to the press) complaining about Clinton's failure, during over twenty hours in the air, to invite Gingrich (and Senate Majority Leader Bob Dole) to the front cabin to talk about the budget deadlock that threatened to shut down the government.

McCurry explained that it would have been unseemly to conduct budget talks during the pre-funeral flight, and that it was almost midnight when the plane headed home. This failed to mollify Gingrich, whose vexation was also inspired by his and Dole's back-of-the-plane seating and their being asked by White House staffers to use the rear door to deplane. The bickering went on for days, with McCurry finally blurting, "Look, Clinton didn't want to schmooze with Gingrich when his friend had just died. Gingrich should just grow up." But nooooo! Instead, Gingrich continued publicly stewing about the "shabby treatment" he'd been subjected to.

"This is petty, and I am going to say up front this is petty . . . but I think it's human," Gingrich told reporters a full ten days after returning home. "You land at Andrews [Air Force Base] and you've been on the plane for twenty-five hours and nobody has talked to you and they ask you to get off the plane by the back ramp." Petty or not, he couldn't stop. "You just wonder, where is their sense of manners? Where is their sense of courtesy? Had they been asleep all night and it hadn't occurred to them that maybe Bob Dole deserved the dignity of maybe walking down the front ramp? Forget me, I'm only the Speaker of the House."

Astonishingly, Gingrich then explained that all the snubbing caused Republicans to send Clinton an extra-tough stopgap spending bill which he vetoed, as they knew he would, resulting in a five-day government shutdown and eight hundred thousand federal workers being laid off because of one man's fit of pique. Clinton said he would apologize "if it would get the government open," but Gingrich dismissed the offer as "irrelevant."

Democrats took to the House floor to ridicule the Speaker. "I was on an airplane and asked for an aisle seat," mocked Illinois representative Luis Gutierrez. "They gave me a window. Then the pilot would not come back and say hello. Then they made me get out of the front of the plane with all the other passengers!" Colorado representative Pat Schroeder said Gingrich should get an Oscar for "best performance by a child actor." Even Republicans piled on, with Kansas representative Pat Roberts dubbing Gingrich "the Rosa Parks of *Air Force One*." (This upset the president of the NAACP, who pointed out that Parks was a hero and Gingrich was not.) In the White House press room, McCurry said, "Maybe we could send [Gingrich] some of those little M&Ms with the presidential seal on it."

And, of course, Gingrich's already low poll numbers plummeted further, because, as could have been predicted, America couldn't have cared less which door he departed the president's airplane from.

——

Furious at what he felt was his inferior seating at a 1994 ceremony breaking ground for New York City's Holocaust memorial, and certain (though wrong) that his nemesis, Mayor Rudy Giuliani, was responsible, New York senator **Alfonse D'Amato** confronted an aide to the mayor and shouted, "I'm a U.S. senator! Who moved my seat?" after which he unleashed a stream of vile profanities.

A VERY WILD ACCUSATION

House Speaker **Dennis Hastert**'s 2004 suggestion that at least part of liberal billionaire George Soros's fortune came from illegal drugs: "You know, I don't know where George Soros gets his money . . . if it comes from overseas or from drug groups or where it comes from." Asked if he was accusing Soros of taking money from drug cartels, Hastert babbled, "Well, that's what he's been for a number of years . . . George Soros has been for legalizing drugs in this country. So, I mean, he's got a lot of ancillary interests out there. I'm saying I don't know where groups . . . could be people who support this type of thing. I'm saying we don't know."

MOST MEMORABLE MELTDOWN

Having lost the 1962 California gubernatorial race, a red-eyed **Richard Nixon** came down the next morning to face the media he so hated. "Now that all the members of the press are so delighted that I lost," he began, proceeding to deliver a rambling harangue in which he said he'd be taking "a long holiday" from politics, and concluding, "Just think how much you're going to be missing. You won't have Nixon to kick around any more, because, gentlemen, this is my last press conference."

14 NOT-QUITE ON-THE-NOSE PROGNOSTICATIONS

Former Rumsfeld and Reagan aide **Kenneth Adelman** wrote a February 2002 *Washington Post* op-ed piece in which he said, "I believe demolishing Hussein's military power and liberating Iraq would be a cakewalk. Let me give simple, responsible reasons: (1) It was a cakewalk last time; (2) they've become much weaker; (3) we've become much stronger; and (4) now we're playing for keeps."

A year later, with the toppling of Hussein's statue, he authored another piece patting himself on the back for his earlier prescience. "My confidence 14 months ago," he wrote, "sprang from having worked for Don Rumsfeld three times—knowing he would fashion a most creative and detailed war plan—and from knowing Dick Cheney and Paul Wolfowitz well for many years."

And three years after that, he devoured a heaping plate of crow, telling *Vanity Fair*, "I just presumed that what I considered to be the most competent national security team since Truman was indeed going to be competent. They turned out to be among the most incompetent teams in the postwar era. Not only did each of them, individually, have enormous flaws, but together they were deadly, dysfunctional."

Widely suspected of infidelity to his wife, Lee, Colorado senator **Gary Hart**, one of the front-runners for the 1988 Democratic presidential nomination, was the subject of a May 1987 *New York Times Magazine* interview in which he challenged reporters, "Follow me around. I don't care. I'm serious. If anybody wants to put a tail on me, go ahead. They'd be very bored."

Reporters from the *Miami Herald* promptly took him up on his dare, staked out his D.C. home, and boredom did not ensue. Instead, they discovered Hart there with Donna Rice, a young woman not his wife. Stories circulated about an earlier Hart–Rice assignation on a boat delightfully named the *Monkey Business*, and by week's end, Hart had dropped out of the presidential race with a bitter blame-the-press diatribe that was so evocative of Richard Nixon's famous "Last Press Conference" that Nixon himself called afterward to assure Hart he'd "handled a very difficult situation uncommonly well."

Hart got back in the race seven months later with the rallying cry, "Let's let the people decide." They did, and he quickly got back out, with his best showing in the primaries being the 7.5 percent of the vote he won in Puerto Rico.

With speculation mounting about whom he would pick as his 1988 running mate, **George Bush** told reporters, "I'll be out at the appropriate time to make that announcement, and it will be laden with suspense . . . and everybody will say, 'What a fantastic choice.'"

—

Immediately following George Bush's selection of Indiana senator J. Danforth Quayle as his vice presidential running mate, Nevada senator **Chic Hecht** exclaimed exuberantly, "He's hot. He's dynamite. Overnight, he'll become a national hero." Overnight, Quayle became a national punchline.

—

Less than forty-eight hours before Hurricane Katrina struck New Orleans, Louisiana governor **Kathleen Blanco** stood in the soon-to-be-wiped-out Jefferson Parish and assured Louisianians, "I believe we are prepared. That's the one thing that I've always been able to brag about."

—

Talking to reporters about the then-three-week-old Monica Lewinsky scandal, **Hillary Clinton** said in 1998, "I don't think this will evaporate, but I anticipate it will slowly dissipate over time, reaching to insubstantiality."

—

Four days after the 1972 Watergate break-in, President **Richard Nixon** and his chief of staff **H. R. Haldeman** were discussing its potential political ramifications. "Anything that's as bizarre as this . . . is going to be a national story," Nixon said. "The reaction is going to be primarily in Washington and not the country because I think the country doesn't give much of a shit about bugging when somebody bugs somebody else, you see. Everybody around here is all mortified about it. 'It's a horrible thing to bug.' Of course it isn't, and most people around the country think it's probably routine, everybody's trying to bug everybody else. It's politics. That's my view.

"Now the purists probably won't agree with that," he summed it up, "but I don't think you're going to see a great, great uproar in the country about the Republican committee trying to bug the Democratic headquarters."

———

Six months before New Orleans flooded, FEMA Director **Michael Brown** declared, "Our nation is prepared, as never before, to deal quickly and capably with the consequences of disasters and other domestic incidents."

———

With the Watergate scandal escalating by the day, the main safety net Richard Nixon had by late 1973 was the grim reality that impeaching him would give the country President **Spiro Agnew**. Then, like a gift from the gods, the vice president's bribe-taking past while governor of Maryland caught up with him, and his legal troubles were suddenly competing with Nixon's for the daily headlines. As the investigations closed in on him and criminal charges seemed imminent, Agnew boldly declared, "I will not resign if indicted! I will not resign if indicted!" Eleven days later, he entered a plea of nolo contendere, or no contest—basically a guilty plea without using that stigmatizing word—to charges of income tax evasion in exchange for the government dropping the bribery charges, and, of course, resigned.

—

Just before the Iraq War began in 2003, **Dick Cheney** asserted, "My belief is we will, in fact, be greeted as liberators." Two years later, George W. Bush said, "I think we are welcomed. But it was not a peaceful welcome."

—

Just before the Iraq War began, Secretary of Defense **Donald Rumsfeld** said, "I can't tell you if the use of force in Iraq today will last five days, five weeks, or five months, but it won't last any longer than that."

—

In 2005, **Dick Cheney** said of the Iraqi rebels, "I think they're in the last throes, if you will, of the insurgency."

—

During a 2000 Republican debate, **George W. Bush** promised, "The administration I'll bring is a group of men and women who are focused on what's best for America, honest men and women, decent men and women, women who will see service to our country as a great privilege and who will not stain the house."

—

Appearing on MSNBC's *Hardball* in 2000, candidate **George W. Bush** assured Chris Matthews, "I understand reality. If you're asking me as the president, would I understand reality, I do."

24 ASSESSMENTS OF CHARACTER PRESERVED THANKS TO **RICHARD NIXON**'S WHITE HOUSE TAPES

Supreme Court Justice Potter Stewart: "A weak bastard . . . overwhelmed by the Washington–Georgetown social set."

—

Supreme Court Justice Hugo Black: "A senile old bastard."

—

Supreme Court Justice William Brennan: "A jackass Catholic."

—

Supreme Court Justice Thurgood Marshall: "An old fool and a black fool."

—

Washington Post publisher Katharine Graham: "She is a terrible old bag."

—

Secretary of State William Rogers: "Rogers is not really smart."

—

Press Secretary Herb Klein: "Klein just doesn't have his head screwed on."

—

Secretary of the Treasury George Shultz: "That candy-ass."

＝

House Whip Tip O'Neill: "An all-out dove and a vicious bastard."

＝

Massachusetts senator Ted Kennedy: "A goddamn lily-livered mealy-mouth."

＝

Sen. Ted Kennedy, again: "And, of course, Teddy. Jesus, he's lighter than the snow . . . and playing around with girls."

＝

Milton Eisenhower (Dwight's brother): "He's a jerk."

＝

Moderate Republican Kentucky senator John Sherman Cooper: "He's an old fart."

＝

West German Chancellor Willy Brandt: "Good God, if that's Germany's hope, Germany ain't got much future. . . . Actually, Brandt is a little bit dumb."

＝

Maine senator Edmund Muskie: "He's not very smart. Clever politically but not smart."

＝

California governor Ronald Reagan: "Reagan, on a personal basis, is terrible. He just isn't pleasant to be around. . . . He's just an uncomfortable man to be around—strange."

＝

Acting FBI Director L. Patrick Gray: "The thick-necked mick."

＝

Judge John Sirica: "The wop judge." Alternatively, "That wop."

＝

Watergate burglar G. Gordon Liddy: "That asshole Liddy."

＝

Canadian Prime Minister Pierre Trudeau: "That asshole Trudeau."

＝

Watergate burglar E. Howard Hunt: "That s.o.b. Hunt."

＝

His brother Donald Nixon: "My damn dumb brother."

＝

The heads of the Securities and Exchange Commission: "Those Jewboys." Or "The S.E.C. Jewboys."

＝

Supreme Court nominee William Rehnquist: "That clown Renchburg."

2 GUYS WHO HAVE A FUTURE WITH THE BAGHDAD CHAMBER OF COMMERCE

New York representative **Peter King** described a 2006 visit to Baghdad as "like being in Manhattan," citing its shopping centers, restaurants, and video stores, as well as its "major hotels" and "bumper-to-bumper traffic," to support his claim that "you would never know there was a war going on." Of course, the occasional "car bomb goes off . . . and at any given time a suicide bomber can walk into an amusement center, but the point I'm making is that the situation is more stable than you think."

Having been soundly mocked for telling an interviewer, "There are neighborhoods in Baghdad where you and I could walk," Republican presidential candidate and Iraq War cheerleader **John McCain** was forced to pay a 2007 visit to the city to prove his point. "Never have I been able to go out in the city as I was today," he said after his stroll, but since he'd been accompanied by twenty-two soldiers and ten armored Humvees and had two Apache helicopters hovering above, the mocking continued unabated.

5 TONSORIAL DISASTERS

Using a blowtorch to sever a steel "ribbon" and formally open the 1972 convention of the American Society of Metals, Cleveland mayor **Ralph J. Perk** managed to set his hair on fire. (Perk attracted the nation's attention again months later when his wife declined a White House dinner invitation on the grounds that it conflicted with her bowling night.)

—

In an effort to appear more youthful than his sixty-eight years, Democratic presidential wanna-be **Alan Cranston** dyed his hair an unfortunate shade of orange in 1982.

—

A $200 haircut by Beverly Hills hairdresser Cristophe given to **Bill Clinton** aboard *Air Force One* in 1993 made his critics giddy when it seemed that several flights had been delayed in connection with the plane sitting on the Los Angeles airport tarmac while the presidential locks were being trimmed. In fact, federal records later showed that not a single scheduled flight was in any way delayed by the incident.

—

In 2007, **John Edwards** repaid his campaign for the 2008 Democratic presidential nomination $800 for two Beverly Hills haircuts.

—

Before he was expelled from the House of Representatives and began serving an eight-year prison sentence in 2002 for all the usual things congressmen go to jail for (bribe-taking, tax evasion, and racketeering), Ohio representative **James Traficant** sported the most ridiculous toupee not just in Congress, but quite possibly in the history of Congress.

TOO LITTLE INFORMATION

When Missouri senator **Thomas Eagleton** was chosen in 1972 to be Democratic presidential nominee George McGovern's running mate, he neglected to mention that he'd been thrice hospitalized for physical and nervous exhaustion and had twice received electric shock treatments. Despite McGovern's pledge of "one thousand percent" support, Eagleton was on the ticket a mere eighteen days before being replaced by Sargent Shriver.

TOO MUCH INFORMATION

Asked at a 1994 MTV town meeting if his preferred underwear was boxers or briefs, President **Bill Clinton** answered, "Usually briefs."

At the 1988 Republican Convention in New Orleans, a reporter for the *Hartford Courant* asked **George W. Bush**, "When you're not talking about politics, what do you and your father talk about?" He replied, "Pussy."

Asked about his habit of keeping a journal recording, in mind-numbing detail, the minutiae of his daily life—really, pretty much everything he does every minute of the day, it's a wonder he has time to actually do anything but write—Florida senator **Bob Graham** said in 2003, "I guess I err on the side of inclusion."

A QUOTE THAT SHOWS HOW WRONG KANYE WEST WAS ABOUT **GEORGE W. BUSH**

"I believe that people whose skins aren't necessarily—are a different color than white—can self-govern." (2004)

4 SKEPTICS SCOFFING

"I can tell you, our grandchildren will laugh at those who predicted global warming," Rev. **Jerry Falwell** opined in 2002. "We'll be in global cooling by then, if the Lord hasn't returned. I don't believe a moment of it. The whole thing is created to destroy America's free enterprise system and our economic stability." According to Falwell, the Earth "is God's planet, and he's taking care of it. And I don't believe that anything we do will raise or lower the temperature one point."

Indiana representative **Earl Landgrebe**, who said in 1974 that Richard Nixon "represented the highest existence of a human being," dismissed the validity of the White House tapes. "There are guys that can talk like Nixon and sound like him," he said, "and I don't even believe the tapes are authentic."

In her successful 1994 campaign for an Idaho congressional seat, antienvironmentalist **Helen Chenoweth** said of her refusal to take the endangered species status of the sockeye salmon seriously, "How can I when you go in and you can buy a can of salmon off the shelf in Albertsons?"

———

Oklahoma senator **James Inhofe**, who called global warming "the greatest hoax ever perpetrated on the American people," confronted Al Gore at a 2007 Senate hearing and told him that scientists are "radically at odds" with the claims made in Gore's Academy Award–winning film, *An Inconvenient Truth*. "How come you guys never seem to notice it when it gets cold?" Inhofe asked, triumphantly brandishing a photograph of icicles in Buffalo, NY. "Where is global warming when you really need it?"

7 UNFORTUNATE PHOTO OPS

President **Lyndon Johnson**, whose lack of boundaries extended to having others follow him into the bathroom and continue conversations or other unfinished business while he defecated, lifted his shirt to display the scar following his 1965 surgery to remove his gall bladder.

———

Longtime Nixon assistant **Rose Mary Woods** twisted herself into a pretzel behind her desk in 1973 to demonstrate how her foot "accidentally" hit a pedal, causing her to "unwittingly" erase 18½ doubtlessly incriminating minutes of a key Watergate-related White House tape.

———

Having just resigned in disgrace with the law at his heels, **Richard Nixon** climbed the steps to the helicopter that would transport him from the White House to his final flight on *Air Force One* to exile in San Clemente, CA, raised both arms, and held up the second and third fingers of each hand in a wildly incongruous V-for-Victory salute.

———

Democratic candidate **Michael Dukakis** attempted to prove his manliness during the 1988 presidential campaign by riding in a tank. The resulting photo of his helmeted head sticking out of the top of the tank with a stupid grin on his face instantly became the gold standard against which all other self-sabotaging campaign photos are judged.

———

With **Gary Hart**'s presidential hopes evaporating in the wake of his having been found alone at home with nonwife Donna Rice, the *National Enquirer* unearthed a photo of her sitting on his lap. "The attractive lady whom I had only recently been introduced to dropped into my lap," Hart explained, adding gallantly, "I chose not to dump her off."

———

As speaker after speaker at the 2004 Republican Convention stood at their podium and said manly things about defending the nation, Democratic nominee **John Kerry** was photographed windsurfing off Nantucket Island.

———

When a reporter suggested that he seemed unenthusiastic after meeting with president Hu Jintao during a 2005 press conference in China, **George W. Bush** snapped, "Have you ever heard of jet lag? Well, good. That answers your question." He then strode hurriedly to a set of double doors, pulled on the handles, and, much to the amusement of the world's press, found the doors locked.

3 GUYS WHO LIKED THEIR SEX PARTNERS YOUNG

In 2004, former Oregon governor **Neil Goldschmidt** confessed that three decades earlier, when he was mayor of Portland, he'd committed statutory rape by starting a three-year-long sexual relationship with his then-fourteen-year-old babysitter.

In 1989, Ohio representative **Buz Lukens** was convicted of contributing to the delinquency of a minor—by paying a sixteen-year-old girl $40 to have sex with him—after a Columbus TV station taped him at McDonald's talking to the girl's mother about the relationship, which was rumored to have started when the girl was thirteen. Though he refused to resign, Lukens failed to win the next year's primary, and distinguished himself as his term wound down by being accused of fondling a Capitol elevator operator.

Florida representative **Mark Foley**—cleverly nicknamed "Foley-man" by George W. Bush—resigned in 2006 after the contents of his lewd instant messages to teenage Congressional pages were exposed. "Did you spank it this weekend?" he asked one boy toy, interrogating him about his masturbation technique ("Where do you unload it?" and "Where do you throw the towel?") while volunteering details of his own ("I always use lotion and the hand"). Sadly, just as things were getting exciting ("get a ruler and measure it for me"), the kid wrote, "brb . . . my mom is yelling."

Oh, and one other sweet detail. In 1998, Foley had said of Bill Clinton's dalliances with Monica Lewinsky, "It's vile. It's more sad than anything else, to see someone with such potential throw it all down the drain because of a sexual addiction."

2 BAD JUDGMENT CALLS

After serving less than three years as a Supreme Court justice—a lifetime position affording him the opportunity to influence the future of the nation—**Arthur Goldberg** resigned in 1965 at President Lyndon Johnson's behest to become ambassador to the United Nations, a position he resigned from three years later in the vain hope of going back to the Supreme Court.

New York governor **Mario Cuomo** turned down President Bill Clinton's offer to be a Supreme Court justice in 1993. He went on to be defeated in the next year's gubernatorial election and pretty much disappeared from public life.

SOME NICER WORDS

In 1982, President **Ronald Reagan** explained that his proposed five-cents-a-gallon gasoline tax "would be a user fee."

＝

Calling it "the right missile at the right time," President **Ronald Reagan** in 1982 renamed the MX "the Peacekeeper."

＝

President **Ronald Reagan** explained that the 1983 U.S. military action in Grenada was not an invasion, it was a "rescue mission."

＝

Alaska senator **Ted Stevens** said of the $23,000 salary increase the Senate voted itself in 1991, "It is not a pay raise. It is a pay equalization concept."

＝

Secretary of State **Condoleezza Rice** began referring to the 2007 troop escalation in Iraq as an "augmentation."

＝

In 2006, **Dick Cheney** referred to the simulated-drowning interrogation technique known as "water boarding" as "a dunk in the water."

＝

During a 2007 TV interview, Homeland Security Advisor **Frances Townsend** called the failure to capture Osama bin Laden "a success that hasn't occurred yet."

9 UNFORGETTABLE DESCRIPTIONS

British Prime Minister Margaret Thatcher said of President **Ronald Reagan**, "Poor dear, there's nothing between his ears."

—

Newsday columnist Murray Kempton wrote of vice presidential candidate **Dan Quayle**, "He is not a ruminating creature. His nesting place is the mindless crowd, and his native woodnote the barbaric yawp. . . . The back of [his] head is beginning to bald and his pale eyes sit upon a balcony of crow's feet and there is the alarming suspicion that he will too soon be wrinkled and yet still be callow and too early grown old before he has really grown up."

—

New York Times columnist Gail Collins wrote of presidential candidate **George W. Bush**, "If Dan Quayle looked like a deer caught in the headlights when he was in front of the cameras, Mr. Bush sometimes resembles a possum cornered in the garage—hunched over, tense, eyes darting worriedly."

—

A 1982 *Los Angeles Times* profile of industrialist and Reagan crony Justin Dart included a scene in which Dart spotted former president **Gerald Ford** on an airplane. After exchanging some genial small talk, Dart returned to his seat and told the reporter, "Gerry's a nice man but he's not very smart. Actually our seatmate is a dumb bastard."

—

In a 1982 essay for *The New Republic,* media analyst Mark Crispin Miller said First Lady **Nancy Reagan** was "glassy-eyed and overdressed" and "always looks as if she has just been struck by lightning in a limousine."

—

A 1988 *Washington Post* editorial said of ethically challenged attorney general **Ed Meese**, "[He] leaves a smudge wherever he goes."

—

In his 1988 autobiography, former Arizona senator Barry Goldwater called **Richard Nixon** "the most dishonest individual I have ever met in my life. He lied to his wife, his family, his friends, his colleagues in the Congress, lifetime members of his own political party, the American people and the world. . . . No lie is intelligent, but his were colossal stupidity because they involved the presidency of the United States."

—

In 1998, New York state Democratic chairman Judith Hope said of Sen. **Alfonse D'Amato**, "He would have a carnival at a Holocaust memorial if he thought it would get him another vote."

—

In 2000, *Washington Post* reporter Robin Givhan said of Florida secretary of state **Katherine Harris**, "Her skin had been plastered and powdered to the texture of pre-war walls. . . . She, to be honest, seems to have applied her makeup with a trowel."

3 MISCONCEPTIONS **PAT ROBERTSON** HAS ABOUT THE FAIRER SEX

"NOW is saying that in order to be a woman, you've got to be a lesbian." (1997)

"[Planned Parenthood] is teaching kids to fornicate, teaching people to have adultery, every kind of bestiality, homosexuality, lesbianism—everything that the Bible condemns." (1991)

"The feminist agenda is not about equal rights for women. It is about a socialist, anti-family political movement that encourages women to leave their husbands, kill their children, practice witchcraft, destroy capitalism and become lesbians." (1992)

6 THINGS VICE PRESIDENT **DAN QUAYLE** DID DURING THE LAST HALF OF HIS TERM

He hailed America's quick victory in Iraq as "a stirring victory for the forces of aggression."

He told a Christian group, "My friends, no matter how rough the road may be, we can and we will never, never surrender to what is right."

He told a New Hampshire audience, "You didn't make a mistake by electing Ronald Reagan in 1980 and 1984, and you didn't make a mistake by electing George Bush in 1988, and you're not gonna make a mistake by electing anyone else besides George Bush in 1992."

He visited a New York hospital and asked administrators if AIDS patients were "taking DDT."

He wrote a column about the 1992 Los Angeles riots that began, "When I have been asked during these last weeks who caused the riots and the killing in L.A., my answer has been direct and simple: Who is to blame for the riots? The rioters are to blame. Who is to blame for the killings? The killers are to blame."

He attacked the sitcom *Murphy Brown*—in which the unmarried main character had a child—as "mocking the importance of fathers," pointing out, "Illegitimacy is something that we should talk about in terms of not having."

THE MOMENT OF PUBLIC STUPIDITY
AGAINST WHICH ALL OTHERS ARE JUDGED

In 1992, Vice President **Dan Quayle** held a spelling bee at a Trenton, NJ, elementary school and told twelve-year-old William Figueroa, who had just spelled "potato" correctly on the blackboard, "You gotta add a little bit at the end there. Spell that again now." When the kid spelled it correctly again, Quayle said, "Now add one little bit on the end. Think of po-ta-to, how is that spelled? You're right phonetically, but what else . . . ?" Figueroa capitulated and stuck an "e" at the end, and Quayle said, "There you go!" Afterward, Figueroa said the incident "showed the rumors about the vice president are true." What rumors? "That he's an idiot."

Predictably, the media's delight in this supreme gaffe pissed off the easily irritated second lady. "He gives five speeches a day for twenty-five months, never makes a mistake," griped **Marilyn Quayle** with astonishing inaccuracy. "He makes one mistake and they air, air, and air it."

4 QUOTES THAT MIGHT WELL LEAD
ONE TO CONCLUDE THAT THE SPEAKER
IS AN INSUFFERABLE HORSE'S ASS

When someone asked **Henry Kissinger** in 1981 if he'd read D. M. Thomas's novel *The White Hotel*, he replied, "I don't read books. I write them."

Four months after Minnesota senator Paul Wellstone was killed in a 2002 plane crash, his successor **Norm Coleman** declared, "To be blunt—and God watch over Paul's soul—I am a 99 percent improvement over Paul Wellstone."

Responding to *Politically Incorrect* host Bill Maher's unpopular observation that the 9/11 hijackers, however crazy they were, did not qualify as "cowards"—and that "We have been the cowards, lobbing cruise missiles from two thousand miles away"— White House spokesman **Ari Fleischer** piously intoned, "The reminder is to all Americans that they need to watch what they say, watch what they do, and that this is not a time for remarks like that. It never is."

Told to put out his cigar in a restaurant in 2003 because of federal government regulations prohibiting smoking there, House Majority Leader **Tom DeLay** shot back, "I *am* the federal government."

FROM THE TANGLED TONGUE OF CHICAGO'S MAYOR **RICHARD J. DALEY**

"We shall reach greater and greater platitudes of achievement."

"They have vilified me, they have crucified me; yes, they have even criticized me."

—

"We are proud to have with us the poet lariat of Chicago."

—

"I resent the insinuendos."

GIDDIEST VICE PRESIDENT

Denying that he and President Reagan disagreed about tax increases as they ran for re-election in 1984, Vice President **George Bush** chirped, "There's no difference between me and the president on taxes. No more nit-picking. Zip-a-dee-doo-dah. Now it's off to the races."

—

Mocking the opposing ticket's refusal to subscribe to the mindless optimism of the Reagan re-election campaign, Vice President **George Bush** said of Walter Mondale, "If somebody sees a silver lining, he finds a big black cloud out there. I mean, right on, whine on, harvest moon!"

—

In 1986, Vice President **George Bush** referred to trouble as "deep doo-doo."

—

After a 1987 tour of the Auschwitz death camp, Vice President **George Bush** enthused, "Boy, they were big on crematoriums, weren't they?"

5 ANGRY MEN

At the 1992 Republican convention, keynote speaker **Pat Buchanan** delivered a harangue exhorting listeners to "take back our cities, take back our culture, and take back our country" from the pro-abortion, pro-gay, pro-pornography types. Columnist Molly Ivins suggested that the speech "probably sounded better in the original German."

———

At the 2004 Republican convention, Democratic Georgia senator **Zell Miller** delivered a keynote speech attacking John Kerry's antidefense voting record. "This is the man who wants to be the commander in chief of the U.S. Armed Forces," he ranted, practically foaming at the mouth. "U.S. forces armed with what? Spitballs?" Later, pissed off at being criticized by Chris Matthews for the tone of his speech, he told the *Hardball* host to "get out of my face" and lamented that we no longer "lived in the day where you could challenge a person to a duel."

———

Upset by 1970 protests on the UC Berkeley campus, California governor **Ronald Reagan** called the demonstrators "cowardly fascists" and said, "If it takes a bloodbath, let's get it over with. No more appeasement."

Four years later, irked that poor people were receiving free food as a result of one of the ransom demands by Patty Hearst's kidnappers, the Symbionese Liberation Army, Reagan huffed, "It's just too bad we can't have an epidemic of botulism."

———

The day before the 1970 Kent State shootings, in which four students at a campus antiwar demonstration were shot to death by National Guardsmen defending themselves against various tossed objects, Ohio governor **Jim Rhodes** said of the big bad protestors, "They're worse than the brownshirts and the communist element and also the nightriders and the vigilantes. They're the worst type of people that we harbor in America. I think that we're up against the strongest, well-trained, militant, revolutionary group that has ever assembled in America."

———

Defending the Bush administration's policy of "extraordinary rendition," in which terrorist suspects are transferred to other countries for interrogation, at a 2007 House hearing, California representative **Dana Rohrabacher** pooh-poohed the notion that it was a big deal if a few innocents were mistreated in order to find the guilty. When spectators began booing this sentiment, he retorted, "Well, I hope it's your families, I hope it's your families that suffer the consequences!"

THE SOUND OF DEMOCRATIC MOMENTUM SCREECHING TO A HALT

Two days after igniting his 1984 presidential campaign by naming the first woman to a national presidential ticket, **Walter Mondale** named Bert Lance—the Carter administration official whose name was most synonymous with "scandal"—as the new Democratic Party chairman.

—

With post-convention polls showing him up as much as seventeen points over George Bush, **Michael Dukakis** took most of the month of August 1988 off, leaving his opponent free to define him as a man who let murderers out of jail and wouldn't allow school kids to say the Pledge of Allegiance.

—

After hanging his 2004 convention acceptance speech on his medal-winning Vietnam experiences, **John Kerry** sat back and did nothing as his war record was trashed by the campaign of a man who not only didn't serve in Vietnam but didn't even fulfill his cushy National Guard service.

MOST PATHETIC COMEBACK TO ACCUSATIONS OF FAILING TO OFFER ANY KIND OF COMEBACK

John Kerry's strategist **Bob Shrum** defended himself against charges that the campaign dawdled in answering the attacks on Kerry's war record by the ludicrously named Swift Boat Veterans for Truth by saying, "We responded within six or seven days."

3 THINGS CANDIDATE **GEORGE W. BUSH** SAID TO REASSURE VOTERS THAT HE WOULDN'T BOTCH THE NATION'S FOREIGN POLICY

"I have had foreign policy as the governor of Texas and that is with Mexico, and I've handled it well."

"I will have a foreign-handed foreign policy."

"The key to foreign policy is to rely on reliance."

7 THINGS **GEORGE W. BUSH** KNOWS ABOUT THE WORLD

"Border relations between Canada and Mexico have never been better." (2001)

—

"There's nothing more deep than recognizing Israel's right to exist. That's the most deep thought of all. . . . I can't think of anything more deep than that right." (2002)

—

"For a century and a half now, America and Japan have formed one of the great and enduring alliances of modern times." (2002)

—

"Europe is America's closest ally." (2005)

—

"Africa is a nation that suffers from incredible disease." (2001)

—

"I understand that the unrest in the Middle East creates unrest throughout the region." (2001)

—

"Iran would be dangerous if they have a nuclear weapon." (2003)

10 TAPED CONVERSATIONS THAT MIGHT LEAD ONE TO BELIEVE **RICHARD NIXON**'S OVAL OFFICE WAS HITLER'S BUNKER

In July 1971, unhappy with the Bureau of Labor Statistics for releasing figures showing rising unemployment, President Nixon asked his aide **Chuck Colson** about the ethnicity of the agency's officials. Colson went through the names, and the president said, "They are all Jews?"

"With a couple of exceptions," Colson said. "You just have to go down the goddamn list and you know they are out to kill us."

Later that same day, the president speculated about members of his National Security Council. "Is [Henry Kissinger's aide] Tony Lake Jewish?" he asked Chief of Staff **H. R. Haldeman**.

"I've always wondered about that," said Haldeman.

"He looked it," the president said. (In fact, he wasn't.)

═══

In 1971, President Nixon, upset with the amount of money Jewish donors were giving to the Democratic Party, told his aide **John Ehrlichman**, "John, we have the power. Are we using it now to investigate contributors to [1968 Democratic presidential nominee] Hubert Humphrey? Contributors to [then front-runner for the 1972 Democratic nomination Edmund] Muskie? The Jews, you know, that are stealing in every direction?"

Days later, the president told Chief of Staff **H. R. Haldeman**, "Please get me the names of the Jews. You know, the big Jewish contributors to the Democrats. . . . Could you please investigate some of the cocksuckers?"

Semites were still on the president's mind the next day. "What about the rich Jews?" he asked **H. R. Haldeman**. "The IRS is full of Jews, Bob." Haldeman suggested finding anti-Semitic IRS workers to audit those rich Jews. Giving this idea his blessing, President Nixon said, "Go after them like a son-of-a-bitch."

When a 1971 *Washington Post* poll showed that 60 percent of the residents of upscale D.C. neighborhoods were against the war, President Nixon had a ready explanation. "There's a hell of a lot of Jews in the District, see," he told **H. R. Haldeman**. "The gentiles have moved out."

Complaining in 1971 that intellectuals—i.e., Jews—on his National Security Council could leak information about the Vietnam War, President Nixon griped to **H. R. Haldeman** that "they will lie, cheat, anything. Basically," he said, summing up, "they have no morals."

"The Jews are all over the government. . . . Most Jews are disloyal," President Nixon told **H. R. Haldeman** in 1971. "I want to look at any sensitive areas where Jews are involved [in the government], Bob. Generally speaking, you can't trust the bastards. They turn on you."

"You know, it's a funny thing," President Nixon said one day in 1971 to **H. R. Haldeman**. "Every one of the bastards that are out for legalizing marijuana is Jewish. What the Christ is the matter with the Jews, Bob? What is the matter with them? I suppose it is because most of them are psychiatrists."

———

In a 1971 conversation, President Nixon was upset about a *Los Angeles Times* story reporting that his nominee for U.S. treasurer, Romana Banuelos, had thirty-six illegal aliens working at a food-processing plant she owned. So the president called Attorney General **John Mitchell** for a little revenge. "There's one thing that I want done and I don't want any argument about it," he barked. "I want you to direct the most trusted person you have in the immigration service, that they are to look over all of the activities of the *Los Angeles Times*. All. Underlined. . . . [Publisher] Otis Chandler, I want him checked with the gardener, his gardener. I understand he's a wetback. Is that clear?"

On a roll now, the president suggested that Chandler's taxes be audited, and that the immigration official who ratted out his treasury nominee be fired for doing his job. **H. R. Haldeman** observed that this official's name, "interestingly, is Rosenberg." Nixon grabbed the phone again and called Mitchell back. "He's a kike by the name of Rosenberg," he crowed. "He is to be out. He is to be out. Get him out. I want his resignation on my desk by the end of the day. Is that clear? Rosenberg is to go. He is to go. I leave it to you to come up with an excuse."

———

Discussing a 1971 *Time* magazine article about the opening of the Kennedy Center in Washington, **H. R. Haldeman** told President Nixon about a series of photos of composer/conductor Leonard Bernstein "kissing everybody he could find and, ah, he's kissing a lot of men on the mouth, you know, including the big black guy. I think it's Alvin Ailey, the head of the dance troupe."

"You know the Jews do that," the president said.

"But not on the mouth!" said Haldeman.

"He did?" The president was stunned. "Kissing on the mouth?"

"Yeah," said Haldeman, "right head on."

"Ah," said President Nixon, "absolutely sickening."

──

One day in 1972, Rev. **Billy Graham** stopped by to visit President Nixon. As it so often did with the president, the conversation quickly turned to the subject of Jews—in this particular instance, his complaint about Jewish domination of the media.

"This stranglehold has got to be broken," the reverend agreed, "or this country's going down the drain."

"You believe that?" the president asked.

"Yes, sir," said Graham.

The president was excited. "Oh boy," he said. "So do I. I can't ever say that, but I believe it."

"No," the reverend said, "but if you get elected a second time, then we might be able to do something."

They spoke briefly of other things, then the president returned to the topic of undue Jewish influence, this time in Hollywood.

"A lot of Jews are great friends of mine," Graham said. "They swarm around me and are friendly to me. Because they know that I am friendly to Israel and so forth. But they don't know how I really feel about what they're doing to this country."

"You must not let them know," the president said, and soon afterward, the reverend departed.

Later, when he was telling **H. R. Haldeman** about Graham's visit, President Nixon said, "You know, it was good we got this point about the Jews across. . . . The Jews are [an] irreligious, atheistic, immoral bunch of bastards."

WHAT **JESSE JACKSON** HAD IN COMMON WITH RICHARD NIXON

During the 1984 Democratic presidential campaign, Rev. Jesse Jackson privately referred to Jews as "Hymie" and called New York "Hymietown." After two weeks of denials, he admitted having said it, though not "in the spirit of meanness."

2 MEMORABLE—IF NONSENSICAL— THINGS **JESSE JACKSON** SAID IN 1984 BESIDES "HYMIETOWN"

"If you deal with text out of context, you have a pretext."

═══

"We are in a different phase now, trying to merge the thesis and the antithesis into a synthesis without doing violence to either."

GREAT NEWS ABOUT AMERICA

"We're no longer a super power. We're a super-duper power."
House Majority Whip **Tom DeLay**, 2002.

BAD NEWS ABOUT AMERICA

"Well, you know, that's the problem with America, we're always having elections."
Texas senator **John Cornyn**, 2006.

A FUNNY MISTAKE

Antichoice Florida governor **Jeb Bush** spent the twenty-sixth anniversary of the Supreme Court's *Roe v. Wade* decision dealing with his campaign's erroneous donation of $10,000 in leftover funds to an Orlando women's health center that often referred clients to abortion clinics. "I want my money back," Bush said, but Tammy Sobiesky, president of the facility, felt no urge to oblige. "I know how he feels about abortion," she said, "but it's not my job to make sure he had his facts straight."

HOW **DICK CHENEY** IS JUST LIKE
THE FOUNDING FATHERS

"You know, the very document that protects our liberties more than anything else, the Constitution, was, of course, drafted in total secrecy."

Ari Fleischer in 2002, defending the administration's refusal to release records of Dick Cheney's energy task force meetings.

RICHARD NIXON TALKS ABOUT CRIME

"People have a right to know if their president's a crook. Well, I'm not a crook." (1973)

—

"Perjury is an awful hard rap to prove." (1973)

—

"When the president does it, that means it is not illegal." (1977)

WHY **TED KENNEDY** COULDN'T FULLY ENJOY THE THRILL OF THE FIRST MOON LANDING IN 1969

He'd driven off the Dike Bridge on Chappaquiddick Island two nights earlier and had failed to rescue the woman in the car with him.

THE HYPOCRITIC OATH

Injecting himself into the 2005 case of severely brain-damaged Terri Schiavo, whose husband had been fighting for years to have her feeding tube removed, Senate Majority Leader **Bill Frist**—a doctor, though not a neurologist—"spent an hour or so looking at" a videotape of Schiavo lying in bed and took to the Senate floor to contest her doctors' diagnosis. "That footage, to me," he pronounced, "depicted something very different than persistent vegetative state." Regardless of what the footage told Frist—he said, "She certainly seems to respond to visual stimuli"—the autopsy confirmed the original diagnosis (and that she was blind), and Frist's presidential ambitions went on life support. The plug was pulled in 2006.

DISORDER IN THE HOUSE

Openly gay Massachusetts representative **Barney Frank** was reprimanded by the House in 1990 after it became known that a male prostitute he'd met through a personal ad was conducting an escort service out of Frank's apartment.

—

After a night of drinking in 1974, Arkansas representative **Wilbur Mills**'s car was pulled over by D.C. police, at which point Fanne Foxe, the stripper he'd been having an affair with—and apparently, that evening, a fight with, since his face was cut—tried to escape by jumping into the Tidal Basin. Though Mills went into rehab (or what passed for rehab in the pre–Betty Ford era), it didn't take, and two months later he turned up drunk onstage during Foxe's performance at a Boston burlesque house.

—

Ohio representative **Wayne Hays** resigned in 1976 after Elizabeth Ray, the mistress he'd hired as his secretary, became upset at not being invited to his wedding to another of his secretaries and itemized her lack of qualifications—"I can't type, I can't file, I can't even answer the phone"—to the *Washington Post*.

—

Addressing a group of Young Democrats in 2003, possibly drunk Rhode Island representative **Patrick Kennedy** declared, "I don't need Bush's tax cut. I have never worked a fucking day in my life," leaving it to members of his audience to ponder how he passed his days on Capitol Hill. "He droned on and on, frequently mentioning how much better the candidates would sound the more we drank," reported someone in attendance. "Finally, he had to be stopped by a DNC volunteer."

Three years later, he crashed his car into a Capitol Hill barricade after narrowly missing a police car in the middle of the night. Given that an officer on the scene said he was staggering and seemed drunk, one might expect his sobriety to have been tested, but as frequently happens with Kennedys and cars, normal laws didn't apply and his blood alcohol levels weren't measured. A stint in rehab followed.

———

Convinced that White House deputy counsel Vince Foster's 1993 suicide was in fact a murder engineered by President Bill Clinton, Indiana representative **Dan Burton** conducted a reenactment in his back yard by firing a handgun into "a head-like object" widely reported to have been a pumpkin.

Two years later, during a 1995 hearing on U.S. drug policy, he suggested that the military should station an aircraft carrier off the coast of Bolivia and crop-dust its coca fields—a difficult task given that Bolivia, entirely surrounded by Argentina, Brazil, Chile, Paraguay, and Peru, has no coast.

———

Wyoming state senator **Barbara Cubin**, elected to Congress in 1994 as the family-values candidate, admitted that she once placed penis-shaped cookies on the desks of her male colleagues, though she took pains to point out that she hadn't baked them herself.

===

Asked by a *Spy* magazine reporter in 1993, "What should the United States do to stop ethnic cleansing in Freedonia?"—a country that exists only in the Marx Brothers movie *Duck Soup*—Florida representative **Corrine Brown** replied, "I think all of those situations are very, very sad, and I just think we need to take action to assist the people."

GEORGE W. BUSH FEELS THE PAIN

"We understand the fright that can come when you're worried about a rocket landing on top of your home." (2007)

"Make no mistake about it, I understand how tough it is, sir. I talk to families who die." (2006)

STUPID IS AS STUPID DOES

In 1974, *New Times* magazine named Virginia senator **William Scott**—the man whose most memorable quote was "The only reason we need zip codes is because niggers can't read"—as the nation's dumbest congressman. Instead of ignoring the attack by a magazine with a relatively small readership, Scott called a press conference to deny the charge, thereby proving it.

===

Asked to cite the highlight of his first year in the Senate, **William Scott** said in 1973, "Being sworn in was perhaps the highlight of the year."

WORST AIM

On a 2006 hunting trip, **Dick Cheney** accidentally sprayed about two hundred shotgun pellets into the face and upper body of fellow hunter Harry Whittington, whose obituary, whatever he'd accomplished in his life or would yet accomplish, had a new opening line.

EVIL LIVES

President **Ronald Reagan** told a 1983 convention of evangelicals that the Soviet Union was "the focus of evil in the modern world . . . an evil empire," in an oration called by historian Henry Steele Commager "the worst presidential speech in history, and I've read them all."

After **George W. Bush** referred to Iran, Iraq, and North Korea as an "axis of evil" in his 2002 State of the Union address, speechwriter **David Frum**'s proud wife, **Danielle Crittenden**, sent out an e-mail claiming credit for him for the phrase. "I realize this is very Washington of me to mention, but my husband is responsible for the Axis of Evil segment," she wrote.

"It's not often a phrase one writes gains national notice . . . so I hope you'll indulge my wifely pride in seeing this one repeated in headlines everywhere." As it turned out, his creation had been "axis of hatred," which speechwriter Michael Gerson changed to "axis of evil," so only two-thirds of the credit was actually Frum's. And as it turned out, George W. Bush was not happy to have people be reminded that the phrase wasn't his own, and Frum was soon an ex–White House speechwriter.

BAD NEWS FROM BEIRUT

Asked about the safety of U.S. Marines in Beirut in 1983, President **Ronald Reagan** said, "We're looking at everything that can be done to make their position safer. We're not sitting idly by." Four days later, a truck bomb in their barracks killed 241 Marines.

After a suicide bomber drove a truck bomb into the U.S. embassy annex in Beirut in 1984, President **Ronald Reagan** justified the fact that an iron security gate was lying on the ground awaiting installation at the time by saying, "Anyone that's ever had their kitchen done over knows that it never gets done as soon as you wish it would." *New York Times* columnist Russell Baker responded, "Anyone that's ever had their kitchen done over knows that the process is nothing at all like trying to stop somebody from driving a truckload of explosives into your house."

3 UNEXPECTED QUERIES

Addressing a fifth-grade class while campaigning in the 2000 New Hampshire primary, rabidly antiabortion presidential hopeful **Alan Keyes** asked the kids, "If I were to lose my mind right now, and pick one of you up and dash your head against the floor and kill you, would that be right?" The class said no. "It's wrong to kill children, isn't it?" Keyes went on. "At what age is it right to kill children? How old are you, son?"

"Eleven," a boy answered. "Think it was okay to kill you when you were six?" Keyes asked. "No," the boy said. Keyes turned to a girl. "How old are you, young lady?" "Ten," she said. "Think it was okay to kill you when you were one?" Keyes asked. She did not.

═

Campaigning in 2004, presidential candidate **John Kerry** responded to the mention of stock car racing by asking, "Who among us does not love NASCAR?"

═

Seeking to establish some male camaraderie before beginning one of his 1977 post-resignation interviews with David Frost, **Richard Nixon** asked him, "Well, did you do any fornicating this weekend?" Said Frost, "It was a mind-boggling moment. It was so touchingly clumsy."

BEST DESCRIPTION OF **RALPH NADER**'S SMUGLY IGNORANT BELIEF THAT THE DEMOCRATS AND REPUBLICANS ARE INDISTINGUISHABLE

Washington Post reporter Dana Milbank wrote, "This is true if you stand far enough away from the two parties—in the same way New York and Tokyo would look similar if you were standing on the moon."

5 LIES **GEORGE W. BUSH** TOLD DURING HIS DEBATES WITH AL GORE

He claimed that in his health care program, prescription drugs would be "an integral part of Medicare," when in fact this would be true only under Gore's plan.

He claimed that the bulk of his tax cuts would go to the poor, when in fact the opposite was true, and he claimed the Gore campaign was outspending the Bush campaign, when in fact the Bush campaign was spending $50 million more.

He claimed that the percentage of Texas kids without health insurance had dropped since he'd been governor, when in fact it had risen, and that the percentage of kids nationally without health insurance had risen under Clinton and Gore, when in fact it had dropped.

3 GUYS NOT OVERLY CONCERNED ABOUT ADHERING TO EVERY LITTLE DETAIL OF THE GENEVA CONVENTIONS

South Carolina representative **L. Mendel Rivers** said that the only person who deserved to be punished for the 1969 My Lai massacre in Vietnam was Hugh Thompson, the U.S. helicopter pilot who tried to stop the slaughter and, when he failed, reported it to his superiors.

With the nation outraged at the 2004 Abu Ghraib scandal, Oklahoma senator **James Inhofe** declared himself "more outraged by the outrage" than he was by the degrading treatment of the prisoners. "They're not there for traffic violations," he sputtered. "They're murderers. They're terrorists. They're insurgents. . . . Many of them probably have American blood on their hands. And here we're so concerned about the treatment of those individuals." Inhofe went on to say that he was "also outraged that we have so many humanitarian do-gooders right now crawling all over these prisons, looking for human rights violations while our troops, our heroes, are fighting and dying."

White House counsel **Alberto Gonzales** said in 2002 that the war on terrorism was "a new kind of war" that "renders obsolete Geneva's strict limitations on questioning of enemy prisoners and renders quaint some of its provisions."

6 THINGS SECRETARY OF DEFENSE **DONALD RUMSFELD** SAID HE DOESN'T DO

"I don't do quagmires."

—

"I don't do diplomacy."

—

"I don't do foreign policy."

—

"I don't do predictions."

—

"I don't do numbers."

—

"I don't do book reviews."

WEIRDEST RESPONSE FROM A CANDIDATE WHOSE RELIGION WAS ALREADY PERCEIVED AS AN ELECTORAL HANDICAP

Asked in 2007 what his favorite novel was, Mormon Republican presidential hopeful **Mitt Romney** named Scientology founder L. Ron Hubbard's *Battlefield Earth*. The Bible, his campaign emphasized repeatedly over the next several days, is his favorite overall book.

A BEAUTIFUL MIND

Explaining in 2003 why she refused to watch coverage of the Iraq War on television, **Barbara Bush**—mother of the guy who started it—said, "Why should we hear about body bags and deaths, and how many, what day it's going to happen, and how many this or what do you suppose? Or, I mean, it's, it's not relevant. So, why should I waste my beautiful mind on something like that?"

ROSIEST COLORED GLASSES

Connecticut senator **Joe Lieberman**, having come in fifth in the 2004 New Hampshire primary with a mere 9 percent of the vote (compared to John Kerry's 39, Howard Dean's 26, Wesley Clark's 13, and John Edwards's 12), declared himself "in a three-way split decision for third place."

In 2003, singer **Britney Spears** said of **George W. Bush**, "Honestly, I think we should just trust our president in every decision that he makes and we should just support that, you know, and be faithful in what happens."

GOV. **GEORGE W. BUSH** TALKS ABOUT THE ECONOMY IN THE YEAR 2000

"It's clearly a budget. It's got a lot of numbers in it."

=

"[Gore's tax plan is] going to require numerous IRA agents."

=

"A tax cut is really one of the anecdotes to coming out of an economic illness."

=

"[Democrats] want the federal government controlling the Social Security, like it's some kind of federal program."

=

"The government is not the surplus's money."

GEORGE W. BUSH EXPLAINS HOW HE'S GOING TO SAVE SOCIAL SECURITY

"All which is on the table begins to address the big cost drivers. For example, how benefits are calculate[d], for example, is on the table; whether or not benefits rise based upon wage increases or price increases. There's a series of parts of the formula that are being considered. And when you couple that, those different cost drivers, affecting those—changing those with personal accounts, the idea is to get what has been promised more likely to be—or closer delivered to what has been promised. Does that make any sense to you? It's kind of muddled. Look, there's a series of things that cause the—like, for example, benefits are calculated based upon the increase of wages, as opposed to the increase of prices. Some have suggested that we calculate—the benefits will rise based upon inflation, as opposed to wage increases. There is a reform that would help solve the red if that were put into effect. In other words, how fast benefits grow, how fast the promised benefits grow, if those—if that growth is affected, it will help on the red." (2005)

GEORGE W. BUSH ON CONSEQUENCES AND THE RAMIFICATIONS OF THE LACK THEREOF

"In my judgment, when the United States says there will be serious consequences, and if there isn't serious consequences, it creates adverse consequences." (2004)

A SEVERELY IMPAIRED IMAGINATION

Testifying before the House budget committee in 2003 just prior to the start of the Iraq War, Deputy Defense Secretary **Paul Wolfowitz** said, "It's hard to conceive that it would take more forces to provide stability in post-Saddam Iraq than it would take to conduct the war itself and to secure the surrender of Saddam's security forces and his army. Hard to imagine."

4 EXAMPLES OF WHAT A DICK
DICK CHENEY IS

Asked about his failure to vote in fourteen of the sixteen elections prior to picking himself as George W. Bush's running mate, Dick Cheney—who didn't even bother to vote for Bush in the 2000 primary—said, "I traveled a great deal. My focus was on global concerns," though his failure to vote absentee was less easily explained.

═══

Questioned about his congressional voting record, which included votes in favor of abolishing the Education Department and defunding the Head Start program, and against a ban on plastic guns that can pass through metal detectors, a ban on "cop killer" armor-piercing bullets, the Clean Water Act, the Endangered Species Act, the Equal Rights Amendment, a school lunch program, a resolution calling on South Africa to free Nelson Mandela, and federal funding for any and all abortions, self-designated vice presidential candidate Dick Cheney grumped, "There's so much time and energy and effort devoted to this kind of trivia."

═══

Asked about his family's donation of a mere 1 percent of their $20 million income to charity, Dick Cheney explained, "That's a choice that individuals have to make, in terms of what they want to do with their resources. It's not a policy question. It's a private matter. It's a matter of private choice."

═══

Describing an incident at his father's 2004 funeral, Ron Reagan said, "Cheney brought my mother up to the casket. . . . She has glaucoma and has trouble seeing. There were steps, and he left her there. He just stood there, letting her flounder. I don't think he's a mindful human being."

DEFINITIVE PROOF THAT THE NEW MILLENNIUM DIDN'T CHANGE **DAN QUAYLE**

Explaining why the Israeli–Palestinian conflict is separate from the "War on Terror," he posed this rhetorical question: "How many Palestinians were on those airplanes on September 9th?"

LONGEST-AWAITED MEA CULPA

In 1987, a fifteen-year-old black girl named Tawana Brawley claimed to have been kidnapped, assaulted, and gang-raped by, among others, a New York City cop. Rev. **Al Sharpton** quickly leapt into the fray, shouting "RACISM!" at every turn, accusing city and state officials of cover-ups, and continuing to defend the girl and her story long after a grand jury—and any sentient human who'd been paying attention—concluded that she'd made the whole thing up. Two decades later, Sharpton—whose actions here earned him the nickname "Al Charlatan"—has yet to apologize, though this hasn't kept him from being taken seriously enough by the media to have mounted, however unsuccessfully, a presidential campaign in 2004.

CONGRESSMAN MOST POSITIVELY IMPACTED BY A TRAGEDY

After four months of relentless media coverage of his affair with missing (later found dead) intern Chandra Levy, California representative **Gary Condit** disappeared from the news on September 12, 2001.

5 THINGS PEOPLE SAID ABOUT IRAQ

Chief of Staff **Andrew Card** explained that the reason the White House waited until after Labor Day 2002 to start the campaign to convince the public that an invasion of Iraq was necessary was, "From a marketing point of view, you don't introduce new products in August."

With the 2003 invasion of Iraq just days away, House Majority Leader **Tom DeLay** said, "Nothing is more important in the face of a war than cutting taxes."

"We know he's been absolutely devoted to trying to acquire nuclear weapons, and we believe he has, in fact, reconstituted nuclear weapons."

Dick Cheney on Saddam Hussein, March 16, 2003.

"I don't know anybody that I can think of who has contended that the Iraqis had nuclear weapons."
　　Secretary of Defense **Donald Rumsfeld**, June 24, 2003.

—

"Well, you can't anticipate everything."
　　Dick Cheney in 2006 on the unexpected Iraq insurgency, three years after having said, "I don't think there was a serious misjudgment here."

3 THOUGHTS ON SEX

During a 1974 congressional hearing about amending the Constitution to reverse the year-old Supreme Court decision legalizing abortion, Minnesota representative **John M. Zwach** opined, "There is a sickness of Americans. They have to have intercourse."

—

In 1976, **Jimmy Carter** told a *Playboy* interviewer, "I've looked on many women with lust. I've committed adultery in my heart many times." The fact that a presidential candidate actually said something about his libido became a major story for weeks.

—

President Clinton's surgeon general **Joycelyn Elders**, who was asked to resign in 1994 after calling masturbation "a part of human sexuality" and suggesting that it be taught in schools, said, "If I could be the condom queen and get every young person in the United States who is engaging in sex to use a condom, I would wear a crown on my head with a condom on it."

2 PUBLIC PRIVATE CONVERSATIONS

While being interviewed on CBS's *Eye to Eye with Connie Chung* just before her son became Speaker of the House, **Newt Gingrich**'s mother, Kathleen, coyly said, "I can't tell you what he said about Hillary." Realizing that this meant she was actually bursting to tell, Chung egged her on. "Why don't you just whisper it to me, just between you and me?"

" 'She's a bitch,' " Ma Gingrich quoted her "Newtie." "About the only thing he ever said about her. I think they had some meeting, you know, and she takes over."

This, of course, infuriated Gingrich, who spent the hours before being sworn in as House Speaker traipsing from one network morning show to the next, griping about the exchange and demanding an apology from CBS for taking advantage of his non-media-savvy mother. He couldn't deny his quote, though, since that would be calling his mother a liar, but his spokesman Tony Blankley told reporters that *he'd* heard Gingrich refer to the first lady "as an extraordinarily able and talented woman."

—

Rita Jenrette was in the process of divorcing former Rep. **John Jenrette**, recently convicted of accepting a $50,000 bribe, when she appeared on Phil Donahue's show in 1981 to alert the public to the fact that there were naked pictures of her in the upcoming issue of *Playboy*. Her plugging was interrupted by an on-the-air phone call from her estranged husband, who just called not to say he loved her but rather to air various grievances, among them that he was "embarrassed" by her *Playboy* spread (as well he might have been, since the accompanying article featured Rita's boastful revelation that they'd once had sex on the steps of the Capitol building). He also expressed unhappiness that she'd cleaned $35,000 out of his checking account, which prompted her to complain about his having stripped their home of $30,000 worth of furniture, cookware, photographs, and silver.

The couple did not reconcile. Rita went on to appear in the films *The Malibu Bikini Shop* and *Zombie Island Massacre*. John—who'd been recorded during the Abscam sting (FBI agents posing as oil-rich sheiks) declaring "I've got larceny in my heart"—went on to prison for thirteen months. In 1988, his larcenous heart got him arrested for shoplifting shoes and a necktie and switching the price tags on a pair of pants and a shirt at a Marshalls department store, and he served another month in jail.

7 COMMENTS FROM PEOPLE IN POWER

"I would have to ask the questioner. I haven't had a chance to ask the questioners the question they've been questioning."

George W. Bush in 2001, on being asked if there was anything he wished he'd asked Labor secretary nominee Linda Chavez, whose nomination was withdrawn when it was revealed that she'd had an illegal alien living in her home.

—

"They're very well-treated down there. They're living in the tropics."

Dick Cheney in 2005, on the conditions at the Guantanamo detainment facility.

—

"Our nation must come together to unite."

George W. Bush, 2001.

—

"[It's] just one of those mysteries."

Porter Goss, on his 2006 resignation after less than two years as CIA director.

—

"Too many good docs are getting out of the business. Too many OB-GYNs aren't able to practice their love with women all across this country."

George W. Bush, 2004.

—

"We won the midterms. This is our due."

Dick Cheney in 2004, responding to the suggestion that the government couldn't afford any more tax cuts for the wealthy.

—

"Her job is . . . to help unstick things that may get stuck, is the best way to put it. She's an unsticker."

George W. Bush, on National Security Advisor Condoleezza Rice, 2003.

MOST SURREAL QUOTE

"That's not the way the world really works any more. We're an empire now, and when we act, we create our own reality. And while you're studying that reality—judiciously, as you will—we'll act again, creating other new realities, which you can study too, and that's how things will sort out. We're history's actors . . . and you, all of you, will be left to just study what we do."

Anonymous Bush administration aide in 2002, explaining to journalist Ron Suskind that he was "in what we call the reality-based community," which the aide defined as people who "believe that solutions emerge from your judicious study of discernible reality."

FASTEST FLIP-FLOP

Facing an investigation into bribery charges, Philadelphia mayor **Frank Rizzo** agreed in 1973 to take a lie detector test, declaring, "I have great confidence in the polygraph. If this machine says a man lied, he lied." This confidence lasted all the way up to the moment that Rizzo failed the test, at which point his new opinion was, "This examination is not worth the paper it's written on."

LEAST OMINOUS WARNING

In 1968, New York representative **Adam Clayton Powell** announced, "I want to say this to you whites in the audience, and whites everywhere, that if you think there were riots after Martin Luther King was killed, this nation won't survive if anything happens to Adam Clayton Powell."

MOST DIFFICULT PROTEST
TO TAKE SERIOUSLY

Taking a stand in 1982 against the placement of a proposed nuclear waste repository in his state, Nevada senator **Chic Hecht** pledged his opposition to any "nuclear suppository."

FREE AS A BIRD

Former Idaho representative **Helen Chenoweth-Hage**, a vehement opponent of government regulation (like, for example, seat belt laws), was killed in a 2006 car accident after being thrown from her vehicle because she wasn't wearing a seat belt.

LEAST INTEGRATED PERSONALITY

"We don't all agree on everything. I don't agree with myself on everything."

    Rudy Giuliani in 2007, on the Republican presidential candidates.

11 MORE ITEMS ABOUT **RICHARD NIXON** TO SATISFY THOSE WHO FEEL THE BOOK HAS BEEN TOO LIGHT ON HIM

Discussing the impact of television on political campaigns in a 1980 TV interview with historian Theodore White, Richard Nixon said, "The main thing is to get a good picture, where you're not wiping your brow." As he said this, he provided a visual example by wiping . . . his upper lip.

━━

Unbeknownst to President Nixon, videotape was rolling as he sat in the Oval Office waiting to deliver his 1974 resignation speech. He was aware, though, that White House photographer Ollie Atkins was snapping away, capturing the moment for posterity. Irritated, Nixon tried to get him to stop. "That's enough!" he barked, telling the TV crew in the room, "My friend Ollie'll be wanting to take a lot of pictures of me. I'm afraid he'll catch me pickin' my nose." Nixon tried to chase Atkins out, but the photographer expected to stay to get the historic after-the-speech shot. "Just take it right now," Nixon said, posing with pages in hand. "This is right after the broadcast, you got it?" thus lying to the bitter end.

———

Four days after the Watergate break-in, President Nixon and **H. R. Haldeman** were discussing whether burglar G. Gordon Liddy was willing to be the fall guy for the fiasco. "He says he is," Haldeman said. "Apparently he's a little bit nuts. . . . He sort of likes the dramatic. He said, 'If you want to put me before a firing squad and shoot me, that's fine.' "

"He's a true believer," the president said, "and we'll take care of him. What the hell? Is the worst that he'd break into the Democratic committee? Christ, that's no blot on a man's record."

The subject turned to the other burglars, four of whom were Cuban exiles, who so bungled the operation that President Nixon felt that no one would believe the White House was involved. "It sounds like a comic opera," he said. "Can you hear the Cubans with their accents?" He then emitted a high-pitched cackle.

———

Having gone on national television and announced the (forced) resignation of his closest aides, **H. R. Haldeman** and **John Ehrlichman**, a drunken President Nixon was feeling sorry for himself for not having been instantly inundated with congratulatory phone calls from members of his cabinet. So he called Haldeman to complain about it, and to ask his now-former chief of staff if he might make some phone calls to get reactions to the speech in which his firing was the big story. "I don't think I can," Haldeman said. "I don't, I don't." The president said he understood.

Then Secretary of State William Rogers called to praise the speech. "That was terrific," he fawned, "really superb."

"What parts did you like, Bill?" the needy president asked.

"I liked all of it," Rogers replied. "I just thought it was great."

Later, *Reader's Digest* CEO Hobart D. Lewis called. "They're great men, but I had to do it," President Nixon said of the firings.

"Well, you're going to miss them," Lewis said.

"Oh well, the hell with missing them," the president said. "You can fill any position, Hobe." Then, one more thought: "Hope you liked 'God bless America' at the end. I believe that, you know, very deeply."

—

In a 1972 conversation with **Henry Kissinger** in which they discussed various scenarios for escalating the Vietnam War, President Nixon caught his national security advisor off guard with a surprise alternative: "I'd rather use the nuclear bomb."

"That, I think, would just be too much," said a doubtlessly stunned Kissinger.

"The nuclear bomb," the president repeated. "Does that bother you? I just want you to think big."

A few weeks later, in another conversation with Kissinger, President Nixon pointed out that the only place the two disagreed "is with regard to the bombing. You're so goddamned concerned about the civilians and I don't give a damn. I don't care."

During the antiwar demonstrations on May Day 1971, President Nixon said he hoped that viewers would be repelled by the televised images of violent, unkempt "hippos" high on "LSC."

Desperately seeking a friendly audience as Watergate sent his approval ratings plummeting, President Nixon headed for still-friendly Tennessee and Nashville's Grand Ole Opry, where he got on stage in 1974 and applied his trademark awkwardness to yo-yo dangling.

President Nixon flew to Paris for President Georges Pompidou's funeral. Momentarily exhilarated by the friendly crowds he no longer encountered in America four months before his resignation, he reacted by exhorting, "This is a great day for France!"

On his historic 1972 trip to China, President Nixon (who observed of the country's most famous landmark, "This is indeed a Great Wall!") also toured a museum. When they came upon an exhibit of ancient jewelry, First Lady Pat Nixon exclaimed, "They must be worth a fortune!"

"You ought to search everybody right now," Nixon advised their guide, "to make sure they don't have anything in their pockets."

Richard Nixon told an interviewer in 1983 that being "the most vilified" American politician "didn't bother me that much, but believe me, it bothered my family."

—

In April 1973, Richard Nixon told **H. R. Haldeman**, "I always wondered about that taping equipment, but I'm damn glad we have it."

JUST SAY NO TO CONSERVATION

Asked in 2001 if **George W. Bush** felt that Americans needed to cut back on their excessive energy consumption, spokesman **Ari Fleischer** said, "That's a big no. The president believes that it's an American way of life, and that it should be the goal of policy makers to protect the American way of life. The American way of life is a blessed one."

3 DEMOCRATIC CONVENTION FIASCOS

Thanks to a frivolous vice presidential roll call that dragged on for hours as more than seventy people (among them Archie Bunker) received votes, 1972 presidential nominee **George McGovern** gave his acceptance speech at 3 A.M. Eastern time—prime time in Hawaii.

—

During his acceptance speech at the 1980 convention, President **Jimmy Carter** delivered a litany of deceased party leaders, culminating with "a great man who should have been president and would have been one of the greatest presidents in history: Hubert Horatio Hornblower!"

This hilarious faux pas was followed minutes later by its visual equivalent, as the traditional balloon drop failed, resulting in a sad drizzle of lonely red, white, and blue spheres that augured anything but well for the fall campaign.

———

A similar balloon drop disaster occurred at the 2004 gathering, when John Kerry's acceptance speech was followed on CNN not by the voices of pundits discussing what they'd just heard, but rather by more than two minutes of increasingly frustrated convention producer **Don Mischer**—unaware that his mike was being transmitted around the world—shouting, "Go, balloons. Go, balloons. Stand by, confetti . . . Keep coming, balloons, more balloons, bring 'em, balloons, balloons, balloons, want balloons, tons of 'em, bring 'em down, let 'em all come. No confetti, no confetti yet, no confetti. All right, go, balloons, go, balloons, we need more balloons. All balloons, all balloons should be going, come on, guys, let's move it. Jesus. We need more balloons. I want all balloons to go, God . . . Go, confetti, go, confetti, go, confetti. I want more balloons. What's happening to the balloons? We need more balloons, we need all of them coming down. Go, balloons, balloons, what's happening, balloons? There's not enough coming down. All balloons, where the hell, there's nothing falling. What the fuck are you guys doing up there? We want more balloons coming down, more balloons, more balloons."

2 ATTORNEYS GENERAL AND THEIR ADVENTURES WITH THE SPIRIT OF JUSTICE

In 1986, **Ed Meese** was photographed in front of the bare-breasted *Spirit of Justice* statue as he accepted his pornography commission's 1,960-page two-volume report on this societal scourge. Included was a 108-page alphabetical listing of magazines (*Big Black Cock, Big Black Jugs, Big Fuckin Tits*), books (*Daddy Tastes So Sweet, Daughter Loves Doggy Fun, Desperately Sucking Teacher*), and movies (*Ladies with Big Boobs, Lesbian Foot Lovers, Little Often Annie*), along with detailed descriptions of the contents ("There are two erect penises lying on her cheek next to her wide open mouth," "He masturbates to ejaculation on her buttocks," "Miss Jones says, 'Put it in, put it in, I want it in when I come' ").

In 2002, the Justice Department spent $8,000 putting drapes in front of the statue so **John Ashcroft** could never again be photographed with its bare breast mocking him above his head.

2 **ARNOLD SCHWARZENEGGER**
MEMORIES ABOUT WOMEN

Recalling his days as a muscle man: "Bodybuilders party a lot, and once in Gold's—the gym in Venice, California, where all the top guys train—there was a black girl who came out naked. Everyone jumped on her and took her upstairs, where we all got together."

—

Recalling a scene in *Terminator 3*: "I saw this toilet bowl. How many times do you get away with this? To take a woman, grab her upside down, and bury her face in a toilet bowl? I wanted to have something floating in there. . . . The thing is, you can do it, because in the end, I didn't do it to a woman. She's a machine! We could get away with it without being crucified by who-knows-what group."

4 FREUDIAN SLIPS

Delivering his farewell speech to the 1988 Republican convention in New Orleans, President **Ronald Reagan** misstated his catch-phrase of the evening, "Facts are stubborn things," as "Facts are stupid things."

—

In what turned out to be the Watergate-besieged president's final State of the Union message, **Richard Nixon** brought up the subject of welfare reform. Though the text of the speech asked Congress to "replace the discredited present system," Nixon said, "I urge the Congress to join me in mounting a major new effort to replace the discredited president."

—

At a visit to Expo '74 in Spokane, President **Richard Nixon** introduced Washington governor Dan Evans as "Governor Evidence."

—

Railing against excessive drug industry profits in 1993, President **Bill Clinton** complained, "The prescription drug industry is spending one billion more dollars a year on advertising than they are on developing new jugs. Er, drugs."

THE SINGLE BEST METAPHOR
IN THE HISTORY OF POLITICS
INVOLVING TOOTHPASTE

In an effort to discourage President Richard Nixon's counsel John Dean from meeting with prosecutors in 1973 about Watergate matters, Chief of Staff **H. R. Haldeman** told him, "Once the toothpaste is out of the tube, it's going to be very tough to get it back in."

7 REVELATIONS IN WASHINGTON MEMOIRS

Michael Deaver's *Behind the Scenes*: During a communion service, **Nancy Reagan** accidentally dropped her wafer into the chalice instead of merely dipping it in. **Ronald Reagan**, who had been told to follow his wife's lead, tossed his in as well. And, in other news, the president seemed to seriously believe that Lincoln's ghost haunted the White House.

—

Donald Regan's *For the Record*: **Nancy Reagan** consulted astrologer **Joan Quigley** before approving her husband's schedule.

—

Larry Speakes's *Speaking Out*: Spokesman Speakes twice made up quotes and attributed them to President **Ronald Reagan**, whose own utterances had been "very tentative and stilted," and once claimed that Reagan had said something that had actually been said by Secretary of State George Shultz during an international crisis because Reagan "had had almost nothing to say."

—

In his memoir *Will*, fanatical Watergate burglar **G. Gordon Liddy** claimed that when he was a boy he burned his hand over an open flame to test his endurance.

—

In his eighth book, *In the Arena*, **Richard Nixon** wrote of his mother, "In her whole life I never heard her say to me or to anyone else, 'I love you.'"

2 BUSHES WHO DIDN'T KNOW TAPE WAS ROLLING

Whispering his analysis of his 1984 debate performance against Geraldine Ferraro to a New Jersey longshoreman while surrounded by reporters, Vice President **George Bush** said,

"We tried to kick a little ass last night. Whoops! Oh, God, he heard me! Turn that thing off!"

———

On an Illinois stop during the 2000 campaign, **George W. Bush** spotted a reporter who had dared to write about him critically. "There's Adam Clymer," Bush told running mate **Dick Cheney**. "Major league asshole from the *New York Times*." "Oh yeah," Cheney agreed, "he is, big time."

LONGEST STRANGEST TRIP

Eldridge Cleaver, the self-proclaimed rapist, attempted murderer, Black Panther Party spokesman, and designer of pants featuring an outer sock for the penis, was a conservative Republican Mormon when he died in 1998.

THE INEBRIATION OF **GEORGE W. BUSH**

In 1994, looking back on his childhood in Midland, Texas, he said, "It was just inebriating what Midland was all about then."

———

In 1994, looking back on his none-too-successful career as an oilman, he recalled, "I became totally inebriated with hitting the big one."

9 EXAMPLES OF WHY IT MIGHT NOT BE AS MUCH FUN TO SIT DOWN AND HAVE A BEER WITH **GEORGE W. BUSH** AS SO MANY PEOPLE SEEM TO THINK IT WOULD

Upset about a 1986 article in which journalist Al Hunt predicted that George Bush would not be the 1988 Republican presidential candidate, George W. Bush defended his father's honor by confronting Hunt in a Dallas restaurant and, in front of his wife and four-year-old son, drunkenly snarling, "You no-good fucking son-of-a-bitch, I will never fucking forget what you wrote."

Richard Ben Kramer's book *What It Takes* contains an anecdote about George W. Bush arriving at the Houston Astrodome for a 1986 playoff game expecting to sit with his parents but finding instead that they and their party were sitting in the owner's box and Bush and his group were seated less prestigiously. Noting that his father's chief of staff, Craig Fuller, was sitting in the owner's box, Bush charged over in a rage. "What's happening?" another of his father's aides asked him, to which Bush shot back, "How the hell would I know? Seats ain't worth a shit. I guess the box got a little crowded. . . . People who think they gotta be here."

Asked if there was anything he regretted about his 2000 primary campaign against John McCain—in which he falsely implied that former prisoner-of-war McCain was weak on veterans' issues and ran radio ads falsely portraying McCain, whose sister had breast cancer, as opposed to funding research about the disease—George W. Bush barked, "Like what? Give me an example. What should I regret?"

—

While playing golf in 2003, George W. Bush brandished his club at reporters as if it was a sword and said, "When I say I'm not answering questions, it means I'm not going to answer questions."

—

During a 2006 press conference, George W. Bush made fun of a reporter—"You gonna ask your question with shades on?" he said—for asking him a question without paying him the respect of taking off his sunglasses. It turned out the reporter wasn't dissing Bush—he was merely legally blind, with a degenerative disease that necessitated his avoiding bright light.

—

During a 2006 visit to a Florida nursing home, George W. Bush made fun of a wheelchair-bound resident—"You look mighty comfortable," he said—for not paying him the respect of standing in his presence.

—

After a CIA underling delivered the August 2001 briefing that warned of an impending terrorist attack, George W. Bush told him, "All right, you've covered your ass now."

—

Asked by Bob Woodward if he'd explained his thinking behind a decision about bombing Afghanistan, George W. Bush snapped, "Of course not. I'm the commander—see, I don't need to explain why I say things. That's the interesting thing about being president. Maybe somebody needs to explain to me why they say something, but I don't feel like I owe anybody an explanation."

—

When Philadelphia writer Bill Hangley shook George W. Bush's hand at a 2001 Fourth of July party and told him, "Mr. President, I hope you only serve four years. I'm very disappointed in your work so far," Bush sneered, "Who cares what you think?"

2 PROUD BOASTS OF IGNORANCE

"Why, I can't even pronounce his name!"

> Country singer **Loretta Lynn**, campaigning in Illinois in 1988 for George Bush, explaining why people shouldn't vote for his opponent Michael Dukakis.

—

"How do they tell the difference? They all look the same to me."

> Mississippi senator **Trent Lott** in 2006, wondering, "Why do they hate each other? Why do Sunnis kill Shiites?"

AN OLD PROBLEM, LONG SINCE REMEDIED

Addressing a 1978 gathering of College Republicans, **Newt Gingrich** told them, "I think one of the great problems we have in the Republican Party is that we don't encourage you to be nasty."

9 COMFORTABLE FOLKS WHO THINK GOD MUST HAVE HATED THE POOR PEOPLE, ELSE WHY DID HE MAKE THEM POOR?

In 1994, Texas senator **Phil Gramm**, who earlier noted that America was "the only nation in the world where all our poor people are fat," dismissed the negative financial impact of a proposed Social Security bill on eighty-year-old retirees, saying, "Most people don't have the luxury of living to be eighty years old, so it's hard for me to feel sorry for them."

—

Denying that President **Ronald Reagan**'s economic policies strongly favored the wealthy, Republican finance chairman **Richard DeVos** said in 1981, "When I hear people talking about money, it's usually people who don't have any."

—

Reagan spokesman **Larry Speakes** said that a 1982 proposal by Ed Meese to tax unemployment benefits would "make unemployment less attractive."

Putting the 10 percent unemployment rate in perspective, President **Ronald Reagan** said, "Just remember, for every person who is out of work, there are nine of us with jobs."

Defending George W. Bush's refusal to roll back his tax cuts for the rich while keeping down spending on childcare for mothers trying to get off welfare, Pennsylvania senator **Rick Santorum** said in 2003, "Making people struggle a little bit is not necessarily the worst thing."

In 1981, California senator **S. I. Hayakawa**—known to colleagues as "Sleepin' Sam" in honor of his having nodded off at his Senate desk—voted against exempting seniors from new limits on food stamp eligibility because "the elderly eat less."

Undersecretary of Housing and Urban Development **Philip Abrams** suggested in 1984 that overcrowded housing was "a cultural preference" of Hispanics. "I'm told they don't mind," he said, "and they prefer, some prefer, doubling up."

Acknowledging that his proposed transfer of federal welfare programs to state governments might well deprive some recipients of adequate benefits, 1976 presidential candidate **Ronald Reagan** advised them, "If a state is mismanaged, you can move elsewhere."

At a 2003 press conference, **George W. Bush** said, "First, let me make it very clear, poor people aren't necessarily killers. Just because you happen to be not rich doesn't mean you're willing to kill."

—

Speaking about the Hurricane Katrina refugees from New Orleans who were huddled in the Houston Astrodome a week after the storm hit, **Barbara Bush** said, "What I'm hearing, which is sort of scary, is that they all want to stay in Texas." (Why this was "scary" she didn't say.) "Everybody is so overwhelmed by the hospitality. And so many of the people in the arena here, you know, were underprivileged anyway, so this," and here she couldn't repress a chuckle, "this is working very well for them."

8 MISSIVES! SENT TO **GEORGE W. BUSH**! (THEN GOVERNOR OF TEXAS!) BY HIS DROOLING FAN **HARRIET MIERS**! (THEN HEAD OF THE TEXAS STATE LOTTERY COMMISSION!) YEARS BEFORE SHE BECAME HIS ALMOST-INSTANTLY-WITHDRAWN SUPREME COURT NOMINEE!

"You are the best!"

—

"Hopefully Jenna and Barbara recognize that their parents are 'cool'—as do the rest of us. . . . The dinner here was great—especially the speech! Keep up all the great work. Texas is blessed!"

—

"I found the dishes delicious and the company most enjoyable. Someday, if I ever cook again, I will try some of the recipes!"

—

"Thank you for taking the time to visit in the office and on the plane back. Cool! Keep up all the great work. The state is in great hands. Thanks also for yours and your family's personal sacrifice."

—

"Great speech! Many good compliments in the audience!"

—

"You and Laura are the greatest!"

—

"The Governor's remarks were great, and I have received many, many compliments. Texas has a very popular Governor and First Lady! Meme Shephard, the little girl to whom the Governor gave his autograph, did not stop talking about her experience and about how wonderful the Governor was for three days. . . . I was struck by the tremendous impact you have on the children whose lives you touch."

—

"You are the best Governor ever—deserving of great respect!"

AN UNEXPECTED BONUS BENEFIT FROM THE WAR ON TERROR

In a 2002 interview with *Runner's World* magazine, **George W. Bush** said, "It's interesting that my times have become faster right after the war began. They were pretty fast all along, but since the war began I have been running with a little more intensity."

WHAT WE TALK ABOUT WHEN WE TALK ABOUT WAR

"I just want you to know that, when we talk about war, we're really talking about peace."
   George W. Bush, 2002.

THE INTERESTING THING—WELL, MAYBE NOT THE MOST INTERESTING THING, BUT INTERESTING NONETHELESS—ABOUT GEORGE WASHINGTON

Showing a reporter around the Oval Office in 2006, **George W. Bush** pointed to a painting and said, "That's George Washington, the first president, of course. The interesting thing about him is that I read three—three or four books about him last year. Isn't that interesting?"

2 GUYS WHO DIDN'T GET
ALL WORKED UP ABOUT THE 1986
ARMS-FOR-HOSTAGES SCANDAL

Asked if it wasn't hypocritical to urge other nations not to ship arms to Iran when the U.S. was doing—albeit covertly—precisely that, Chief of Staff **Donald Regan** replied, "Hypocrisy is a question of degree."

Vice President **George Bush**, who, as president, pardoned those convicted in connection with the scandal, said, "On the surface, selling arms to a country that sponsors terrorism, of course, clearly, you'd have to argue it's wrong, but it's the exception sometimes that proves the rule."

2 NONRECURRING ROLES

Former president **Gerald Ford** and **Henry Kissinger** appeared as themselves on a 1983 episode of *Dynasty*, where Kissinger exchanged suggestive dialogue with Joan Collins.

WHY 4 PEOPLE WHO SENT, OR SUPPORTED THE SENDING, OF OTHER PEOPLE'S KIDS TO FIGHT UNWINNABLE WARS DIDN'T FIGHT IN ONE WHEN THEY HAD THE CHANCE

Explaining why—even though he supported the Vietnam War—he used a series of student deferments to avoid serving there, Texas senator **Phil Gramm** said, "As a twenty-six-year-old Ph.D. in economics, I could have quit my job at [Texas] A&M and joined the army. I would have probably ended up working in some library somewhere or maybe teaching at West Point or working in the Pentagon. But I thought what I was doing at Texas A&M was important."

Interim UN Ambassador **John Bolton**, whose rudeness qualified him as an "undiplomat," wrote in his Yale 25th Reunion Book, "I confess I had no desire to die in a Southeast Asian rice paddy. I considered the war in Vietnam already lost."

Dick Cheney, who got five different deferments to keep out of Vietnam, explained, "I had other priorities in the sixties than military service."

"So many minority youths had volunteered," explained Texas representative **Tom DeLay**, "that there was literally no room for patriotic folks like myself."

2 THOUGHTS ON THE 1999 COLUMBINE HIGH SCHOOL MASSACRE

Scoffing at gun-control advocates, House Majority Whip **Tom DeLay** declared, "Guns have little or nothing to do with juvenile violence. The causes of youth violence are working parents who put their kids into daycare, the teaching of evolution in the schools, and working mothers who take birth control pills."

—

Appearing on CNN's *Crossfire*, **Dan Quayle** advised parents, "If you see a sawed-off shotgun or whatever else laying around the house, take it away."

BILL CLINTON CHANNELS DAN QUAYLE

Presidential candidate Bill Clinton told students at the University of Florida that the U.S. "is still the greatest country in the world if we just will steel our wills and lose our minds."

—

Criticizing Republicans for their antigovernment stance at a 1996 Santa Ana, CA, campaign rally, President Bill Clinton said, "They set it up as the enemy. It's government versus the people. The last time I checked, the Constitution said, 'of the people, by the people, and for the people.' That's what the Declaration of Independence says." In fact, it's what Lincoln's Gettysburg Address said.

2 QUOTES GUARANTEED TO APPEAR IN THE UTTERER'S OBITUARY

"It depends what the meaning of the word 'is' is."

President **Bill Clinton** explaining in 1998 that when he said, "There is no sexual relationship" with Monica Lewinsky, he was telling the truth because it had ended months earlier.

—

"I actually did vote for the $87 billion before I voted against it."

2004 presidential candidate **John Kerry**, justifying having voted for the Iraq War but later voting against a bill to fund it.

2 CLUES AS TO WHY MUCH OF AMERICA DISMISSES THE POLITICAL VIEWS OF ACTORS

With President Bill Clinton's impeachment imminent, actor **Alec Baldwin** went on *Late Night with Conan O'Brien* and unleashed a rabid tirade against House Judiciary Committee Chairman (and impeachment leader) Henry Hyde. "If we were in other countries, we would all right now, all of us together, all of us together would go down to Washington and we would stone Henry Hyde to death! We would stone him to death!" Baldwin ranted. "We would stone Henry Hyde to death and we would go to [the homes of pro-impeachment representatives] and we'd kill their wives and their children. We would kill their families!" The audience cheered.

——

At a 2004 salute to John Kerry in New York, **Whoopi Goldberg** made vagina jokes about George W. Bush—get it?

AN OMEN

As the 2000 campaign got under way, computer programmer Zack Exley bought the domain name www.gwbush.com, and created a parody of the **George W. Bush** campaign's Web site. The Bush campaign freaked out, worrying that people could be easily confused that this was Bush's official site, though the headline "Just Say No to Former Cocaine User for President" would certainly seem to have tipped the satirist's hand.

Also featured was an initiative called "Amnesty 2000," through which Bush would pardon those convicted of drug-related crimes if they'd "learned from their mistakes," and fun was made of his self-characterization as a "compassionate conservative," pointing out that "G.W. Bush has indeed been forgiven again and again by others. First there was his rambunctious youth. Then, as an unsuccessful Texas businessman, he was bailed out with millions of dollars from friends of his vice president father. As president, G.W. Bush wants to create an America in which everyone gets as much forgiveness and as many chances to grow up as he had."

The Bush campaign complained to the Federal Election Commission but failed to shut the site down. In fact, the publicity their whining about it created brought the site more than six million hits over a twenty-five-day period during which the actual Bush site got about thirty thousand hits. "There's a lot of garbage in politics, and, obviously, this is a garbage man," an extremely unamused Bush said of Exley, huffing foreshadowingly that "There ought to be limits to freedom." This quote was quickly incorporated into the parody site, which began describing Bush as "the only candidate with the courage to take on excessive freedom on the Internet." Within months, the site featured animation of Bush with a straw up his nose inhaling white lines, and streamed video footage of him picking his nose at a Texas Rangers game.

HOW THE INTERNET WORKS, AS TOLD BY ALASKA SENATOR **TED STEVENS**

"The Internet is not something you just dump something on. It's not a truck. It's a series of tubes. And if you don't understand, those tubes can be filled and if they are filled, when you put your message in, it gets in line and it's going to be delayed by anyone that puts into that tube enormous amounts of material, enormous amounts of material." (2006)

3 TRUTH-STRETCHERS

"I don't know whether he really ran over toward second base and made a one-hand stab or whether he just squatted down and took the ball when it came to him. But the truth got there and, in other words, it can be attractively packaged."

President **Ronald Reagan** in 1982, recalling his days as a sportscaster who made up details of the games to better entertain radio audiences.

—

"If you tell the same story five times, it's true."

Reagan spokesman **Larry Speakes** in 1983, defending his boss's repeated telling of a heroic World War II story that didn't really happen.

—

"See, in my line of work you got to keep repeating things over and over and over again for the truth to sink in, to kind of catapult the propaganda."

George W. Bush in 2005, trying in vain to sell his Social Security program.

MOST LOYAL—TO THE POINT OF LUNACY—NIXON SUPPORTER

In early August 1974, the transcript was released of a two-year-old White House conversation proving that President **Richard Nixon** had been involved in the cover-up of the Watergate break-in from the start. Nixon's congressional support crumbled to dust, as all the House Judiciary Committee members who had recently voted against impeachment reversed themselves. Still, not everyone was convinced. "I'm going to stick with my president," declared Indiana representative **Earl Landgrebe**, "even if he and I have to be taken out of this building and shot."

The next day, Republican congressional leaders went to the White House to tell Nixon it was time to stop being president. Landgrebe, though, was not about to let a little thing like overwhelming evidence of guilt cause him to abandon Nixon. "Don't confuse me with the facts," he said. "I've got a closed mind."

MORE **LANDGREBE**

He was the only congressman ever to vote no on a quorum call. He later said he had a good reason for doing it, which he could no longer recall.

He was the only congressman to vote against funding for cancer research. Why? "We all have to go sometime."

HAPPIEST MUG SHOT

Having stepped down from his position as House majority leader in 2005 after becoming the first congressional leader in history to be indicted, **Tom DeLay** slapped a big grin on his face while being booked for conspiracy and money laundering. "I said a little prayer before I actually did the fingerprint thing, and the picture," he explained. "And my prayer was basically: 'Let people see Christ through me. And let me smile.'"

3 SIMPLE SOLUTIONS TO
SERIOUS PROBLEMS

In a 2007 speech, **George W. Bush** said, "I mean, people have access to health care in America. After all, you just go to an emergency room."

=

President **Gerald Ford** suggested that an effective way to fight the inflation raging through the economy in 1974 was to sport buttons with the acronym "WIN" exhorting fellow citizens to "Whip Inflation Now."

=

Instead of ever asking Americans to make any kind of sacrifice to support the idiotically named "War on Terror," **George W. Bush** repeatedly urged everyone to "go shopping."

HOW WE CAN HELP THE WAR EFFORT
BESIDES BUYING STUFF

"People say, 'How can I help on this war against terror? How can I fight evil?' You can do so by mentoring a child; by going into a shut-in's house and say 'I love you.' By running a Boy Scout troop or a Girl Scout troop, by being involved in your Boys and Girls Clubs, by joining the USA Freedom Corps. If you're interested in helping America fight evil, love your neighbor just like you'd like to be loved yourself."
    George W. Bush, 2002.

BUT WHAT ABOUT THE CONCEPT OF SACRIFICE?

"I think a lot of people are in this fight. I mean, they sacrifice peace of mind when they see the terrible images of violence on TV every night. When you think about the psychology of this country, it is somewhat down because of this war."

George W. Bush, 2007.

A CHRISTMAS CARD THAT COULD ONLY HAVE COME FROM **THE QUAYLES** (OR, AS THEIR NAME WAS SPELLED ON THEIR MAILBOX, "THE QUAYLE'S")

"May our nation continue to be a beakon of hope to the world."

2 INANIMATE OBJECTS THAT WILL ALWAYS MAKE US THINK OF **BILL CLINTON**

Cigars and stained blue Gap dresses

HOW MUSIC COULD HAVE CHANGED THE WORLD, BUT ULTIMATELY DIDN'T

Richard Nixon, in one of the taped reminiscences featured at the Richard Nixon Library and Birthplace in Yorba Linda, CA, shared this little-suspected alternate scenario: "I have often thought that if there had been a good rap group around in those days, I might have chosen a career in music instead of politics."

2 MOST IRONIC CAMPAIGN SLOGANS, GIVEN WHAT HAPPENED AFTER THE ELECTIONS

Richard M. Nixon in 1968: "Bring Us Together."

George W. Bush in 2000: "A Uniter, Not A Divider."

2 "COMEDY" BITS

At the 2004 Radio and TV Correspondents Association dinner, **George W. Bush** narrated a slideshow in which he purported to be searching for the weapons of mass destruction he used as a fake excuse to initiate the colossal fiasco in Iraq. As images of him peeking behind drapes and under furniture appeared on the screen, Bush—blissfully oblivious to the feelings of the families of those who lost life and limbs because of his fraudulent war—joked, "Those weapons of mass destruction have got to be here somewhere. . . . Nope, no weapons over there. Maybe under here." The shamelessly sycophantic correspondents howled.

―

At the 2007 Radio and TV Correspondents Association dinner, **Karl Rove** performed an act consisting of the porcine "Turd Blossom" (his Bush nickname) clumsily gyrating while "rapping" jokes about his hobby of "tearing the tops off small animals"—appropriate humor for the chief adviser to George W. Bush, who, as a boy, blew up frogs with firecrackers—while repeating the refrain, "I'm MC Rove." The shamelessly sycophantic correspondents not only howled but two of them, NBC's David Gregory and Ken Strickland, got on stage and merrily joined in this hideous display.

4 CLUES THAT **GEORGE W. BUSH** FINDS IT AMUSING WHEN PEOPLE DIE

When a debate moderator in 2000 brought up an incident in which the lawyer for a death-row inmate slept through much of his client's trial, Bush's response was to chuckle.

―

When he told a 2000 debate audience about what was going to happen to the psychos who dragged a black man to death behind a truck—"Guess what? The three men who murdered James Byrd, guess what's going to happen to them. They're going to be put to death"—Bush had a big smile on his face.

===

In a 1999 interview with Tucker Carlson for *Talk* magazine, he recounted an appearance by condemned killer Karla Faye Tucker on *Larry King Live.* "He asked her real difficult questions, like, 'What would you say to Governor Bush?'" And what was her response? Bush pursed his lips in mock desperation and whimpered, " 'Please don't kill me.'" As grotesque as this would have been if she'd actually pleaded for her life, the ugliness of it given that she never said any such thing takes one's breath away.

===

Seconds before he went on television in 2003 to announce that the United States was at war with Iraq, he pumped his left fist and said, "I feel good." MSNBC's Chris Matthews pronounced himself struck by Bush's "almost giddy readiness to kill."

SOMETHING THAT **CONDOLEEZZA RICE** SAID COULDN'T HAVE BEEN FORESEEN THAT ACTUALLY HAD BEEN, AND MORE THAN ONCE

"I don't think anybody could have predicted that these people would take an airplane and slam it into the World Trade Center, take another one and slam it into the Pentagon, that they would try to use an airplane as a missile."

National Security Advisor Condoleezza Rice, May 16, 2002.

Nobody, that is, except the French intelligence officials who thwarted a 1994 terrorist plan to slam a plane into the Eiffel Tower, and the intelligence officials who prepared a 1999 study warning that a "suicide bomber belonging to al-Qaeda's Martyrdom Battalion could crash-land an aircraft packed with high explosives . . . into the Pentagon, the headquarters of the CIA, or the White House," and the FBI agent who urged an investigation into the number of Arab men enrolled in American flight schools, and the CIA officials who delivered, on August 6, 2001, the White House briefing paper none too cryptically headlined, "Bin Laden Determined to Strike in U.S.," and the FBI agent who tried to get someone to take seriously his warning about a man who offered a Minnesota flight instructor thousands of dollars to learn how to steer—but not land—a jumbo jet. But, aside from them, nobody.

SOMETHING THAT **GEORGE W. BUSH** SAID COULDN'T HAVE BEEN FORESEEN THAT ACTUALLY HAD BEEN, AND MORE THAN ONCE

"I don't think anybody anticipated the breach of the levees."
George W. Bush (who'd been playing guitar in San Diego with country singer Mark Willis as the floodwaters drowned New Orleans), on *Good Morning America*, September 1, 2005.

Nobody, that is, except Louisiana State University scientists (whose computer model runs, two days before Hurricane Katrina made landfall, had indicated precisely that eventuality), the Federal Emergency Management Agency (which warned, that same day, that the storm "could greatly overtop levees and protective systems"), and the Department of Homeland Security's National Infrastructure Simulation and Analysis Center (which e-mailed a forty-one-page paper to the White House crisis center the day the storm struck, predicting "severe flooding and/or levee breaching"). But, aside from them, nobody.

GAYEST STATEMENT BY THE NOT-GAYEST SENATOR EVER TO GET HIMSELF ARRESTED IN AN AIRPORT MEN'S ROOM FOR GAY BEHAVIOR AND PLEAD GUILTY TO THE CHARGE DESPITE NOT BEING, AND NEVER HAVING BEEN, GAY

During a 1999 appearance on *Meet the Press*, Idaho senator **Larry Craig** said of the possibility of censuring the president, "The Senate certainly can bring about a censure resolution, and it's a slap on the wrist. It's a, 'Bad boy, Bill Clinton. You're a naughty boy.' The American people already know that Bill Clinton is a bad boy, a naughty boy. I'm going to speak out for the citizens of my state, who in the majority think that Bill Clinton is probably even a nasty, bad naughty boy."

THE 4 GREATEST QUOTES OF
THE NEW MILLENNIUM

"There are some who feel like the conditions are such that they can attack us there. My answer is 'Bring them on.'"

> **George W. Bush** in 2003, thinking he was displaying his *cojones* but actually inviting Iraqi insurgents to attack our troops.

=

"I don't think America can stand by and hope for the best from a madman."

> **George W. Bush** in 2004, thinking he was talking about Saddam Hussein.

=

"Sometimes leaders show up who do a great disservice to the traditions and people of a country."

> **George W. Bush** in 2006, thinking he was talking about Venezuelan President Hugo Chavez.

=

"I'm optimistic because I believe I'm right. I'm at peace with myself."

> **George W. Bush** in 2003, brushing off the urgings of Spain's prime minister, Jose Maria Aznar, to "have a little patience" before barging into Iraq.

INDEX

A NOTE ON THE AUTHOR

Paul Slansky is the author of *The Clothes Have No Emperor* and *The George W. Bush Quiz Book*, and the coauthor of *My Bad: The Apology Anthology* and *Dan Quayle: Airhead Apparent*. He is a frequent contributor to the *New Yorker* and the *Huffington Post*, and his work has also appeared in, among dozens of publications, the *New York Observer*, *Spy*, the *New York Times Magazine*, the *New Republic*, *Newsweek*, *Esquire*, *Playboy*, *Rolling Stone*, *ForbesLife*, and the *Soho News*. He lives in Los Angeles.